MW01222803

BIBLICAL SOLUTIONS
FOR
DAILY LIVING

DEVELOPING A VITAL AND
PERSONAL RELATIONSHIP WITH GOD

Aleta You, PhD

Scriptures quoted throughout the book are from the King James Version unless otherwise noted. The Greek and Hebrew words are italicized and their translations have been obtained from *Young's Analytical Concordance to the Bible* (Michigan: William B. Erdmans Publishing Company, 1970). When Holy Spirit is capitalized, it refers to the giver, God. When holy spirit is lower case, it refers to the gift. Explanatory insertions within a scripture are enclosed in brackets.

Photo by Karen McLean
Cover design by Inkroots Corporation

Copyright © 2014 Aleta You
All rights reserved.
ISBN: 1490303693
ISBN-13: 9781490303697
Library of Congress Control Number: 2013912421
CreateSpace Independent Publishing Platform
North Charleston, South Carolina

That I may publish with the voice of thanksgiving,
and tell of all thy wondrous works.
Psalm 26:7

TO MY PARENTS

Eleanor Soonie Chun You

For teaching me the importance of prayer and believing in God

Richard Wonsang You

For teaching me, by example, about the power of positive believing

KIRKUS INDIE REVIEW

Approaching religion with an academic sensibility, this auto-biographical guide advocates the Bible as a text for intensive study, one to be regularly revisited by the faithful.

With a background in traditional Western philosophy, You develops her spiritual guide as a supplement to the postdoctoral academics that left her hungry for true wisdom . . . You demonstrates the breadth of her biblical knowledge by referencing numerous, often lesser-known stories from the Bible, including Asa as proof that God protects loyal followers and Abigail to show the benefits of trusting God completely . . . You generally elucidates the significance of *"what a person chooses to believe"* over the mere fact of whether a person has faith . . . You's friendly tone evokes small-group study, more personable than a pastor preaching from the pulpit...

A detailed . . . guide to Scripture for daily study and devotion, sidestepping sanctimony in favor of thoughtful tips and reader-friendly resources.

FOREWORD

This intelligent book weaves classical philosophy and litera- ture into an understanding of how the Bible reveals the na- ture of God.

In *Biblical Solutions for Daily Living: Developing a Vital and Personal Relationship with God,* Aleta You, PhD, provides a well-researched and accessible guide for practical uses of the Bible. Through personal testimony, prose, and exercises designed for additional study, You successfully demonstrates the importance and relevance of the Bible for everyday life.

You begins with a personal narrative. At an early age, she starts on a quest to understand the nature of God. As an adult, she stud- ies philosophy and different religions and also faces personal chal- lenges. Through these experiences, she comes to the conclusion that the Bible is a gift provided by God to understand God's true nature. In the text, You presents this argument with support in the form of scripture.

Subsequent chapters describe the attributes of God, the com- petition between good and evil on the personal and spiritual plane, the importance of the Holy Spirit, and the usefulness of the Bible for good health and creating a mind/body balance. All of the chapters include personal testimony at the beginning and end,

as well as a set of thought-provoking questions and a list of biblical passages for further exploration. You also seamlessly weaves in
her understanding of philosophy and the classics to exemplify her
points.

Biblical Solutions for Daily Living provides a comprehensive anal-
ysis of a complex text. You points out that many people feel the
Bible is important yet have not read it; as such, the purpose of
her book is to encourage biblical literacy. You includes biblical
passages from the Old and New Testaments, drawing inspiration
from Psalms, Proverbs, and the Gospels and addressing the Book
of Revelation. All of the information is presented in well-orga-
nized sections.

Though the volume's language is accessible to a broad audience, its message is specifically for evangelical Christians and others who believe that the Bible is the inerrant word of God . . . A
level of biblical understanding and an appreciation of the Bible are
prerequisites for fully embracing You's arguments.

You presents the culmination of her spiritual journey to form
a personal relationship with God. *Biblical Solutions for Daily Living*
provides the tools necessary for the formation of a spiritual practice including biblical study. Clergy, lay leaders, and Bible study
facilitators will consider this book an important resource.

Gabrie'l Atchison,
Clarion Review

CONTENTS

ACKNOWLEDGMENTS

The idea for this book had been floating around in my head for quite some time. Were it not for the encouragement of a dear friend and a former colleague, Arlene Chasek, I doubt that this book would ever have been written. I am grateful to Arlene for her encouragement, patience, editing, and feedback in helping me see this project through to completion.

I also wish to thank Ann Ware, Ellen Schwartz, Sheri Hizny, Cathy Hobbs, and Jeanette Green for their editorial suggestions and helpful comments. I believe my writing has improved as a result of the many suggestions I received on different versions of the manuscript. If there are any errors, I take full responsibility for them. I would also like to express my gratitude to the talented team at CreateSpace for their assistance in the editing, the interior design and layout, and to David Ogunrinde of Inkroots Corporation for the cover design of the book.

The guidance and prayers of a number of individuals have strengthened and sustained me in my own spiritual growth and development. I am grateful to Reverend Rosalie F. Rivenbark, Reverend and Mrs. Michael Anderson, Reverend and Mrs. John Chelar, Reverend and Mrs. Eric Koetteritz, Reverend and Mrs. Vern Edwards, Reverend and Mrs. David Lippold, Jerry and Robin Weller, Stephen and Michelle Hyder, John Paul and Ilda Recinto, and Tom and Melody Nelson for their believing prayers. My deep appreciation and thanks are also extended to the Board of Directors of The Way International for allowing me to quote from their publications. I want to thank my sisters in Christ Karen Turner, Sonia Pravasi, Marilyn McKie, and the believers in the Body of Christ for their prayers and encouragement throughout this process. Finally, I would like to thank my children, family, students, colleagues, and friends for enriching my life in more ways than they can imagine. Thank you all for being a part of my life and for your love, friendship, and support.

CHAPTER ONE

INTRODUCTION

I don't remember exactly when I learned about God. It may have been when I attended Sunday school as a little girl. Or perhaps I learned how important God was when I saw my mother praying during times of great distress. I soon found myself praying to God for the largest and, at times, the most seemingly insignificant things in life.

I remember in fourth grade when I prayed that I wanted the most popular boy in class to like me. At other times, I remember praying for world peace and for God's protection over my family, friends, and country.

I knew that I loved God, and even though I didn't always get an immediate answer to my prayers, I continued praying and believed in my heart that God heard my prayers. I remember finding a Bible in our home when I was about ten years old. I read a scripture that said, "Verily, verily, I say unto you, He that believeth on me, the works that I do shall he do also; and greater works than these shall he do; because I go unto my Father" (John 14:12). In my child-like innocence, I believed that scripture, but I didn't fully understand its significance until years later.

As a young girl, I began a spiritual journey in wanting to know God's will for my life. Growing up in Honolulu, Hawaii, as a fourth-generation American of Korean ancestry, I was exposed to the rich diversity of cultures, traditions, and religions of many people. Although I was raised as a Christian, I was taught, by the example of my parents, to respect the religions of others even though their beliefs differed from my own.

My mother was a stay-at-home mom who taught Sunday school at our local Methodist church. She had a great zest for life and a deep, abiding faith in God. My father wasn't a particularly religious man in the traditional sense of the word. However, he was an extremely compassionate and caring individual. As a physician and surgeon, he took care of many people. In some instances, if a person couldn't afford to pay his medical bill, my father would not charge the patient for his services. My father believed it was important for people to get the medical care they needed, whether they could afford it or not.

Growing up in a multicultural community, I would often go out with my friends to a *Bon* dance. The *Bon* dance took place at a traditional Japanese festival held during the summer as a memorial service to Japanese people's ancestors. In the midst of colorful paper lanterns swaying gently in the breeze and women dressed in beautiful silk kimonos, my friends joined in the festivities by dancing in a circle. They tried to persuade me to join them, but I was always too shy to participate. Many of my friends had mini-shrines in their homes, with fresh fruit to honor their deceased relatives. It was common for my Buddhist friends to also celebrate Christmas during the holidays.

I vividly remember riding the bus home from school every day and seeing the nuns in their crisp white uniforms, standing outside the hospital. At the time, I contemplated becoming a nun, as I thought it would bring me closer to God. I eventually learned that serving God is not confined to joining an order and that I could love and serve God in other ways.

In college and graduate school, I studied philosophy and learned that *philosophy*, in Greek, means "the love of wisdom." In my naiveté, I thought surely I would find God through the study of philosophy and Eastern religions. Although I loved philosophy as an academic discipline, the search for God and experientially knowing Him as a loving, heavenly Father still eluded me.

One particular event stands out during my undergraduate years at a university in Illinois. I was invited to attend a meeting where a Christian woman gave a powerful sermon. I don't remember exactly what she spoke about except that at the end of her talk, she asked who wanted to be saved and accept Jesus Christ as their Lord and Savior. Whatever she said moved me, and I and several others in the room raised our hands. That evening, I had an amazing dream in which I saw a beautiful dove, surrounded by a brilliant light, descend on me. I remember opening my eyes, thinking that it was a dream, but the same vision remained for a few seconds. In that instant, I was enveloped by a profound sense of peace and love. It brought tears to my eyes as I thought about how much God loved and cared for me, that He gave His Son to wash away all my sins.

The next day, I went to a Christian bookstore and purchased a Bible and started reading the book of John. My roommate remarked that I must have "gotten religion" when she saw the Bible and a picture of Jesus in our room. I didn't care what she or anyone else thought because no one could deny what I had experienced the previous evening. As I began reading the Bible, there were passages that I still didn't understand, and I yearned to learn more about God and His will for my life.

After I graduated from Bradley University, I returned home, married my college sweetheart, and obtained a master's degree in speech communication at the University of Hawaii. My husband was commissioned in the United States Air Force and we moved to Arizona where he began his pilot training at Williams Air Force base.

While living in Arizona, I decided to pursue a PhD in philosophy of education at Arizona State University. I defended my dissertation and our son was born in June of that year. As rewarding as graduate school was in acquiring worldly knowledge, there was still a spiritual emptiness in my heart that needed to be filled with the light of God's Word.

Following my completion of graduate school, my husband received orders for San Antonio, Texas and I accepted a position as assistant professor in an education department at a private college. I taught undergraduate and graduate courses in education and in the social and philosophical foundations of education, and I directed the student teaching program. In addition to my full-time faculty and administrative positions, I enrolled in additional graduate courses in philosophy and also studied Theravāda Buddhism at the University of Texas at Austin. In my search for spiritual understanding, I began reading New Age books. Desiring to see God's power in my life, in my ignorance and desperation, I even consulted a psychic! He charged sixty dollars an hour and required cash up front. Other than listening to him describe a few things about my mother and myself (both of which were inaccurate), I found the whole ordeal to be unfulfilling. Instead of leading to enlightenment, the psychic and the New Age books that I read brought greater confusion and frustration. Little did I know that God was protecting me from the devilish influences of this psychic and the New Age literature.

During this period of my life, I was busy publishing, teaching, directing a student teaching program, raising our son, and fulfilling the responsibilities of a military wife and mother. My hard work in my professional career paid off, and I was promoted to associate professor with tenure. During this hectic time, I became pregnant with our second child and gave birth to a beautiful baby girl in 1979.

From all outward appearances, it looked like I was living the American dream. I was married to an air force pilot, had two beautiful, healthy children, a lovely home, a great job, and a PhD in an academic area that I loved. What more could I ask for? And yet, deep down inside, the spiritual emptiness gnawed at me, telling me that something was still missing in my life. I wanted to experientially know God. I could never forget what took place that evening several years earlier when I accepted Jesus Christ as Lord and Savior in my life. Don't misunderstand me. Getting born again is definitely a big deal. No amount of money can purchase eternal life. However, what was missing was a knowledge and understanding of what this meant spiritually and what was available to me as a born-again believer who received God's incorruptible seed, the gift of holy spirit.

My husband's next air force assignment was to have taken us to Hickam Air Force Base in Honolulu, Hawaii. A paradise assignment! I was ecstatic, and my parents were overjoyed. The air force moved all of our household goods and our car to Hawaii. I had two job offers, and we were all set to fly to my birthplace. Two weeks before our departure, the air force changed my husband's orders and informed us that we would be going to McGuire Air Force Base in New Jersey.

The disappointment was overwhelming. I rationalized that for some reason, God wanted us to move to New Jersey and not Hawaii. The purpose for this change in plans eluded me. My mother's response, when I broke the heartbreaking news to her was, "Where's New Jersey?" For all she knew, it was at the other end of the world.

Like a good military family, we quickly adapted to this change and took what was left behind from the movers and drove to New Jersey. We found a home in South Jersey and slept on the floor for several months. Our household goods had already been sent to Hawaii, and by slow boat, they turned around and eventually found their way to New Jersey. I was depressed at the thought of knocking on doors all over again looking for a teaching position in my field. Our son experienced difficulty adjusting to his new surroundings. He missed his friends in San Antonio and I felt guilty we had put him through this traumatic ordeal.

Finally, one day I had a heart-to-heart talk with God (one of many throughout my life). I wanted answers and wanted to know what His will was for my life. A thought came to me to invite my chiropractor's wife out to lunch. Learning to listen to that "still, small voice" I contacted her and she agreed to meet me for lunch. Over lunch I began pouring my heart out to her and shared my frustration in wanting to know God and His will for my life. "What you want," she said, "can be found in our home Bible fellowship where the Word of God is taught and classes are available to learn God's Word." The year was 1984. As I began attending a Bible fellowship and learned to apply the principles that were taught from the Bible classes, I learned that God's Word works!

In 1985 I accepted a fulltime position as assistant director in the Teacher Preparation Program at Princeton University. A year later, I was offered and accepted a position as project director, overseeing a statewide demonstration program at Rutgers, the

State University of New Jersey. I have been a senior administrator at Rutgers from 1986 till my retirement in July 2013. Beginning with my position at Princeton University in 1985, I was primarily supported by federal, state, and foundation grants. Believing God for His prosperity and protection has been and continues to be a reality in my life.

A great deal of time has passed since my initial thirst for God was met by going to His written Word and finding answers to my prayers. After twenty-nine years of marriage, my husband and I divorced when I discovered his infidelity. My children are now adults and survived their own personal challenges of adolescence. They found their way after a fractured marriage nearly destroyed their self-esteem and trust in what they, and others, thought was a perfect marriage. Regardless of how painful our personal challenges are, I learned that God is always there as we seek Him to strengthen, guide, and lead us out of depression, despair, loneliness, anger, bitterness, betrayal, and any other negative experiences and destructive emotions we may experience in life. In time, God's love can and will heal a broken heart.

The biggest lesson I learned, as a result of studying the Bible, is that we are in a spiritual competition and we don't wrestle against flesh and blood but "against principalities, against powers, against the rulers of the darkness of this world, against spiritual wickedness in high places" (Ephesians 6:12). And yet, in spite of our formidable spiritual enemy, God has fully equipped us with all that we need to stand and withstand against our spiritual adversary, the Devil.

This book reflects a spiritual journey in seeking to learn more about God by studying the Bible and discovering *Biblical Solutions for Daily Living—Developing a Vital and Personal Relationship with God.* In spite of all the academic degrees I acquired, I discovered that learning God's Word, the Bible, brought the greatest amount of peace, joy, satisfaction, knowledge, enlightenment, and power in my life. By God's grace and mercy, the Word of God literally saved my life.

Studying and learning God's Word is an exciting adventure. Growing in spiritual maturity requires decision, commitment, and faithfulness. God doesn't expect us to be perfect. He just asks that we be faithful in our desire to know and live the Word. "A faithful man shall abound with blessings" (Proverbs 28:20).

It is my hope and prayer that this book will encourage you to begin to enjoy reading the Bible and that God will enlighten your eyes of understanding to "know what is the hope of his calling, and what the riches of the glory of his inheritance in the saints" (Ephesians 1:18).

> *And what is the exceeding greatness of his power to us-ward who believe, according to the working of his mighty power.*
> Ephesians 1:19

> *According as his divine power hath given unto us all things that pertain unto life and godliness, through the knowledge of him that hath called us to glory and virtue.*
> 2 Peter 1:3

CHAPTER TWO

THE BIBLE AS THE STANDARD

He sent his word, and healed them, and delivered
them from their destructions.
Psalm 107:20

"Why did God make bad guys?" my son innocently asked when he was six years old. At the time, I was unable to adequately answer his question. Now, as a result of studying the Bible, I have learned to distinguish between the nature of good and the existence of evil.

With the aftermath of September 11, 2001, many today are searching for answers to explain the diabolical attacks waged against our country. In the words of Lisa Beamer, whose husband died as one of several heroes on United Airlines Flight 93, "The evil hearts and minds of those who plotted against us on September 11 will never be understood."[1]

I believe Socrates was correct when he said that "the unexamined life is not worth living." We must search for answers to understand good and evil. Philosophers have debated about the nature of good versus evil since antiquity. Movies and books have been written about the "dark side" and the eternal conflict between these two forces.

THE BIBLE AS THE FRAMEWORK

Did you know that, although approximately 92 percent of Americans own a Bible, and two-thirds say that it holds the answers to the basic questions of life, biblical illiteracy is rampant? Less than half of Americans can name the first book of the Bible, and only one-third knows who delivered the Sermon on the Mount. "We revere the Bible but we don't read it," according to George W. Gallup.[2]

Since September 11, sales of Bibles are up 42 percent, and attendance at churches, synagogues, and mosques is up 5–10 percent. People are interested not only in finding answers to life's perplexing questions but are also interested in understanding the nature of evil.[3]

E. W. Bullinger, a biblical scholar wrote, "The Root of all the evils which abound in the spiritual sphere at the present day lies in the fact that the Word and the words of God are not fed upon, digested, and assimilated, as they ought to be."[4] True wisdom comes from knowing and applying the Word of God.

God desires that we come to know Him as our heavenly Father and that we have a personal, intimate relationship with Him. God cares about every single detail of our lives. One way to know God is to study His Word. Second Timothy 2:15 states, "study to shew thyself approved unto God, a workman that needeth not to be ashamed, rightly dividing the word of truth."

The Bible is an Eastern book, rich with Orientalisms and figures of speech.[5] Learning to read the Bible builds our understanding and provides us with a deeper knowledge of God's message to His people. The Bible is God's love letter to His children.

In my spiritual growth and development, I discovered that the Bible is a steady anchor in the turbulent seas of life. There were times when I was drowning from the pressures of the world. Juggling a career and raising a family, being a wife, mother, chauffeur, cook, and cleaning lady were overwhelming. Reading God's Word gave me guidance, strength, and peace to handle the daily pressures of life.

"Thou wilt keep him in perfect peace, whose mind is stayed on thee: because he trusteth in thee" (Isaiah 26:3). As we stay our minds on God and His Word, He will give us perfect peace. The prophet Jeremiah proclaimed his love for God's Word in the following passage: "Thy words were found, and I did eat them; and thy word was unto me the joy and rejoicing of mine heart" (Jeremiah 15:16).

When the Apostle Paul and Silas traveled to Berea, they observed that the believers were known for their study of the Scriptures: "These were more noble than those in Thessalonica, in that they received the word with all readiness of mind, and searched the scriptures daily, whether those things were so" (Acts 17:11).

BENEFITS OF READING THE BIBLE

Reading the Bible daily will yield great benefits as you learn to retain God's Word in your mind and apply these principles in your life. What are some of the benefits of reading the Bible?

- Increase your positive believing to receive the blessings from God.

- Develop confidence that God is real and He will perform no less than what He says in His Word as you take the believing action.
- Discover that the Bible has answers to all things that pertain to life and godliness.
- Acquire spiritual food for believing images of victory.
- Experience peace in knowing that God is your sufficiency and He will take care of your every need.
- Strengthen your prayer life for yourself, your family, your community, your country, and the world.
- Walk with greater power in your life.

Studying the Bible helps us to contrast what the Bible says with the negative headlines flooding the world. Headlines screaming about global conflicts, the rise and fall of the stock market, skyrocketing debt, terrorist threats, and unemployment are just a few examples of conditions that are not conducive to a peaceful mind. Is it possible to maintain a peaceful mind in spite of the negative circumstances in the world? The answer is a resounding yes! Learning how to focus our minds and claim the promises in the Bible helps to relieve the anxiety and stress of what the world offers. This is not to suggest that we bury our heads in the sand and ignore world events. In spite of the circumstances, it is available for us to renew our minds to what the Bible says and to become Word-conditioned and not circumstance-oriented. The Bible is the antidote to a society that exploits and preys on peoples' fears and insecurities. The Chicken Littles of the world would have us believe that the sky is falling. But is it really?

Understanding biblical research principles allows us to separate truth from error and rightly divide the word of truth (2 Timothy

2:15).[6] Second Peter 1:20 states, "no prophecy of the scripture is of any private interpretation." We are not to privately interpret God's Word with our own opinions. Rather, we are to study and diligently read the Bible in order to understand what God is communicating to us by researching the Scriptures.

David writes in Psalm 138:2 that God has magnified His Word above all His name. This is the high esteem with which God regards His written Word.

In Paul's second epistle to Timothy he writes, "All scripture is given by inspiration of God, and is profitable for doctrine, for reproof, for correction, for instruction in righteousness: That the man of God may be perfect, throughly furnished unto all good works" (2 Timothy 3:16–17).

Inspiration means "God-breathed." All scripture was written by holy men of God who were moved by the gift of holy spirit (2 Peter 1:21). God wants us to grow in the knowledge and understanding of His written Word so we can apply it in our lives and reap the benefits. In spite of the ten plagues afflicting the Egyptians in the Old Testament, there was still light in the land of Goshen and the Israelites were not harmed as long as they obeyed Moses, the man of God who spoke God's Word (Exodus 8:22, 10:23).

As much as I would love a vaccine for instant enlightenment, I learned that understanding the Bible is a long-term process that requires decision, commitment, and faithfulness. God is patient and longsuffering. He knows we are not perfect. However, what He does honor is faithfulness. We are reminded that "the effectual fervent prayer of a righteous man availeth much" (James 5:16) and that "a faithful man shall abound with blessings" (Proverbs 28:20).

God can only give us what we are capable of receiving. Believing the Word of God and being born again of holy spirit requires that we earnestly desire to seek God and His will for our lives. "But without faith [believing] it is impossible to please him: for he that cometh to God must believe that he is, and that he is a rewarder of them that diligently seek him" (Hebrew 11:6).

God rewards us with abundant blessings as we seek His guidance in our lives. Spiritual knowledge is not for the fainthearted. "For every one that useth milk is unskilful in the word of righteousness: for he is a babe. But strong meat belongeth to them that are of full age, even those who by reason of use have their senses exercised to discern both good and evil" (Hebrews 5:13–14).

The Bible builds strength in our lives as we grow in spiritual maturity in our daily walk with God. The Bible is the critical filter that assesses all codes of conduct and is the sieve by which we separate good from evil. Hebrews 4:12 describes the power and benefits of understanding God's Word by stating, "For the word of God is quick, and powerful, and sharper than any two-edged sword, piercing even to the dividing asunder of soul and spirit, and of the joints and marrow, and is a discerner of the thoughts and intents of the heart." God's Word is the litmus test by which we distinguish between good and evil.

The Word of God has great power to transform lives. Believing and acting upon God's Word helps us to make spiritually wise decisions. There are a number of records in the Gospels where Jesus discerned the true intentions of the religious leaders of his day. Instead of rejoicing that Jesus healed a man with a withered hand, due to jealousy and envy, the Pharisees held a council to plan how they might destroy Jesus (Matthew 12:9–15). He accurately discerned the thoughts of the Pharisees and escaped from their treacherous plans to kill him.

NATION FOUNDED ON
BIBLICAL PRINCIPLES

Our nation was founded on biblical principles. The preservation of our government is dependent upon an informed citizenry.[7] Colonial children were taught to read the Scriptures as part of their curriculum. The first textbook for children was *The New England Primer*, which taught children both the ABCs and moral lessons about life through biblical truths. Many of our oldest and most esteemed universities such as Harvard, William and Mary, Yale, Princeton, King's College (Columbia University), Brown, Rutgers, and Dartmouth were founded by Christian preachers and church affiliations.[8]

The national motto of the United States of America, adopted by Congress on July 30, 1956, states, "In God We Trust." Although there was and continues to be an attempt to delete the phrase, "under God," in the Pledge of Allegiance, most Americans want to keep the words in the pledge.[9] When we obey and perform the precepts from the Bible, God is able to bless and protect us from our enemies. "Blessed is the nation whose God is the Lord; and the people whom he hath chosen for his own inheritance" (Psalm 33:12). Conversely, "the wicked shall be turned into hell, and all the nations that forget God" (Psalm 9:17).

In the words of Benjamin Franklin, "We have been assured, Sir, in the sacred writings, that except the Lord build the house they labor in vain that build it. I firmly believe this, and I also believe that without His concurring aid we shall succeed in this political building no better than the builders of Babel."[10]

The Declaration of Independence is the first civil document that recognizes God, rather than a pope or a monarch, as the giver of rights. The founders wrote the following in the second paragraph of the Declaration of Independence: "We hold these Truths to be self-evident, that all men are created equal, that they are endowed by their Creator with certain unalienable Rights, that among these are Life, Liberty, and the Pursuit of Happiness..."[11]

Abraham Lincoln had this to say about the Bible: "In regard to this Great Book, I have but to say, it is the best gift God has given to man. All the good the Savior gave to the world was communicated through this book."[12]

Regardless of our political affiliations, the Bible exhorts us to pray for the leaders of our country.

> *I exhort therefore, that first of all, supplications, prayers,*
> *intercessions, and giving of thanks, be made for all men;*
> *For kings, and for all that are in authority; that we*
> *may lead a quiet and peaceable life in all godliness and*
> *honesty.*
> 1 Timothy 2:1–2

PRACTICAL KEYS TO APPLYING THE BIBLE

1. Begin reading the Bible at least five minutes a day. You can start with Ephesians, a great revelation given to the church. Increase the time to twenty minutes a day.

2. Look up the scriptures listed in this chapter and below for further study. For a more in-depth meaning of the scriptures, use the *Amplified Bible*. Additional Bible versions include the *New American Standard Bible* and the *New International Version* of the English Bible translation.

3. As you prepare to read the Bible, ask God to show you what you need to learn from His Word.

4. Enroll in a Bible class that teaches you biblical principles in understanding the Bible.

SCRIPTURES FOR FURTHER STUDY

Proverbs 3:5–6
Psalm 37:1–9
Psalm 84:11
Psalm 103:1–12

CHAPTER THREE

ATTRIBUTES OF GOD

For the Lord God is a sun and shield: the Lord
will give grace and glory: no good thing will he
withhold from them that walk uprightly.
Psalm 84:11

When I was growing up, my vision of God was that He was a personal being who cared about my life. In my conversations with others, I learned that people from different religions had different images of God, and their perceptions determined their relationship with the Almighty. My God is the God of Abraham, Isaac, and Jacob and the Father of our Lord Jesus Christ.

OTHER GODS

As I began studying the Bible, I discovered there were cultures that believed in more than one God. This is an important distinction, because the Bible describes other gods whom people worshipped. In Genesis 35:2, God exhorts the Israelites, "Put away the strange gods that are among you, and be clean, and change your garments."

Moses cautioned the children of Israel to "have no other gods before me" and to avoid making graven images or bow down and worship them (Exodus 20:3).

The idols of the heathen are silver and gold, the work of men's hands.
They have mouths, but they speak not; eyes have they, but they see not;
They have ears, but they hear not; neither is there any breath in their mouths.
They that make them are like unto them: so is every one that trusteth in them.
Psalm 135: 15–18

Graven images and idols are not the only things that are detestable to the one true God. Anything placed above God is a form of idolatry. This includes your job, money, relationships, sex, material objects, power, worldly knowledge, or self.

Mortify therefore your members which are upon the earth; fornication, uncleanness, inordinate affection, evil concupiscence, and covetousness, which is idolatry:
For which things' sake the wrath of God cometh on the children of disobedience:
In the which ye also walked sometime, when ye lived in them.
But now ye also put off all these; anger, wrath, malice, blasphemy, filthy communication out of your mouth.
Lie not one to another, seeing that ye have put off the old man with his deeds;

And have put on the new man, which is renewed in
knowledge after the image of him that created him.
Colossians 3:5–10

GOD FIRST

Matthew 6:33 states, "But seek ye first the kingdom of God, and his righteousness; and all these things shall be added unto you." When God is given first priority in our lives, blessings abound. God, as the giver of all that is good, continually seeks to bless our lives with health and prosperity. Studying the Bible enables us to identify and claim all that God has richly blessed us with. We just need to recognize what God's blessings are in order to appropriate them.

For those who argue against the existence of God, the Bible clearly states in Psalm 53:1, "the fool hath said in his heart, There is no God. Corrupt are they, and have done abominable iniquity: there is none that doeth good."

Believers of the Bible are not defense attorneys for God. We need not defend or justify God's Word or His existence. God simply is. When Moses said unto God, "When I come unto the children of Israel, and shall say unto them, The God of your fathers hath sent me unto you; and they shall say to me, What is his name?," God replied, "I AM THAT I AM...I AM hath sent me unto you" (Exodus 3:13–14). "I AM" is a name that denotes the unsearchableness of God. God would be whatever Moses needed Him to be to lead the Israelites out of the bondage of Egypt.

God does not change. The God who helped Moses lead the Israelites out of Egypt is the same God that will meet your need according to His written Word. Jesus taught this truth in the Gospel of Luke 11:9–13:

*And I say unto you, Ask, and it shall be given you; seek,
and ye shall find; knock, and it shall be opened unto you.
For every one that asketh receiveth; and he that seeketh
findeth; and to him that knocketh it shall be opened.
If a son shall ask bread of any of you that is a father, will
he give him a stone? or if he ask a fish, will he for a fish
give him a serpent?
Or if he shall ask an egg, will he offer him a scorpion?
If ye then, being evil, know how to give good gifts unto
your children: how much more shall your heavenly Father
give the Holy Spirit to them that ask him?*

I learned this truth firsthand. One of the greatest concerns I
had during and after my divorce was whether I would be able to
make it on my own financially. I had to rely on God to supply
my financial need to pay my attorney fees, living expenses, and
support our children through college. As I tithed and abundantly
shared of my finances to the ministry that taught me God's Word,
I discovered that God was never late in supplying my need.

Psalm 111:10 states, "the fear of the Lord is the beginning
of wisdom: a good understanding have all they that do his commandments: his praise endureth for ever."

Fear comes from the Hebrew word *yare,* and it means "to reverence or respect." God wants us to love, reverence, and respect
His Word and seek His will so that we can live a life of abundance
and power.

WHAT GOD IS NOT

Words are limited in describing God. How does one describe
the infinite in finite terms? To clarify any misconceptions we may

have acquired over the years, we turn to the Bible to learn what God is not.

GOD DOES NOT TEST US

The Trials of Job

An erroneous assumption is that God "tests" us when illness, disease, or tragedy strikes our lives. An illustration of how one man stood against the attacks of the Devil is the story of Job. Job's fear that his sons may have sinned in their hearts against God opened the door for the Devil to attack and kill his children, livestock, and servants (Job 1:1–22). Eliphaz, one of Job's miserable comforters, accused Job unjustly of somehow being responsible for the evil that had befallen his family. Eliphaz erroneously attributed the death of Job's children, his servants, and his livestock to the "chastening of the Almighty" (Job 5:17). Other miserable comforters included Bildad the Shuhite and Zophar the Naamathite. In spite of the verbal attacks of his so-called friends, the death of his children, the destruction of all that he owned, being stricken with boils from the soles of his feet to the top of his head, and his wife admonishing him to "curse God, and die" (Job 2:9), Job held fast to his righteousness by standing up to his miserable comforters: "God forbid that I should justify you: till I die I will not remove mine integrity from me. My righteousness I hold fast, and will not let it go: my heart shall not reproach me so long as I live" (Job 27:5–6).

The Israelites were not aware of a spiritual adversary, as Jesus Christ's ministry had not yet taken place. Job laments, "Oh that one would hear me! behold, my desire is, that the Almighty would answer me, and that mine adversary had written a book" (Job 31:35). God's archenemy, the Devil, will never write a book, because the secret of his success is the secrecy of his moves. God has given us His written Word, and the gift of holy spirit, in order to expose the snares of the Devil. In the end, Job held fast to his righteousness and never blamed God for the calamities that occurred in his life. God blessed Job by giving him twice as much as he had before. Job lived to be one hundred and forty years old and lived to see four generations of his grandchildren.[1]

As we faithfully love God and believe and apply biblical principles in our lives, we too, can look forward to living a long and prosperous life and enjoy the lives of our children and several generations of our grandchildren.

GOD DOES NOT LIE

Numbers 23:19 says that "God is not a man, that he should lie." God's Word is true, and "every one of thy righteous judgments endureth for ever" (Psalm 119:160). What God says in the Bible from Genesis through Revelation is true whether people believe it or not. When apparent inconsistencies or contradictions occur, it is due to people's private interpretation and not rightly dividing the Scriptures (2 Timothy 2:15).

GOD DOES NOT CAUSE SUFFERING

Another misconception about God is that He causes suffering. In the Old Testament the Israelites attributed, and even people today may attribute, both good and evil to God. When a personal challenge occurs in your life, have you ever wondered, "Why is this happening to me?" or "What have I done to deserve this?" When a tsunami, tornado, or earthquake hits, and people are killed, insurance companies call this "an act of God." When loved ones perish in an airline crash or in a collapsing building struck by terrorists, people ask, "If God is all-powerful and merciful, why does He allow this to happen?" God never overrides free will. Evil exists. The Bible says, "many are the afflictions of the righteous: but the Lord delivereth him out of them all" (Psalm 34:19).

When Jesus Christ appeared, he exposed the Devil, our spiritual adversary, as the source of all evil: "He that committeth sin is of the devil; for the devil sinneth from the beginning. For this purpose the Son of God was manifested, that he might destroy the works of the devil" (1 John 3:8). The Bible declares that "God is light, and in him is no darkness at all" (1 John 1:5). "For thou art not a God that hath pleasure in wickedness: neither shall evil dwell with thee" (Psalm 5:4). Furthermore, "every good gift and every perfect gift is from above, and cometh down from the Father of lights, with whom is no variableness, neither shadow of turning" (James 1:17).

In contrast, "They are of those that rebel against the light; they know not the ways thereof, nor abide in the paths thereof. The murderer rising with the light killeth the poor and needy, and in the night is as a thief" (Job 24:13–14).

In spite of the evil and suffering that exists, it is comforting to know that "the Lord redeemeth the soul of his servants: and none of them that trust in him shall be desolate" (Psalm 34:22).

GOD DOES NOT KILL

Many mistakenly attribute death to the one true God. This belief is contrary to what the Bible teaches. John 10:10 says, "the thief cometh not, but for to steal, and to kill, and to destroy: I am come that they might have life, and that they might have it more abundantly." The thief represents our spiritual adversary, the Devil. Whenever there is stealing, killing, or destruction, the Devil is at work behind the scenes. The adversary uses people, culture, and the environment as conduits to promote the systematizing of error by causing confusion, chaos, and evil destruction in the world.

First Corinthians 15:26 says that "the last enemy that shall be destroyed is death." Death is never a friend but is an enemy. The phrase, "I am come," in John 10:10b, refers to Jesus Christ, the only begotten Son of God, whom God raised from the dead. Jesus Christ came that we might have life and have it more abundantly.

GOD DOES NOT TEMPT PEOPLE

God never tempts people. "Let no man say when he is tempted, I am tempted of God: for God cannot be tempted with evil, neither tempteth he any man: But every man is tempted, when he is drawn away of his own lust, and enticed. Then when lust hath conceived, it bringeth forth sin: and sin, when it is finished, bringeth forth death" (James 1:13–15).

It is absurd to assume that if a person smokes cigarettes and is stricken with lung cancer, God somehow caused this disease. Many blame God for the illnesses, maladies, and tragedies in their lives.[2] God never usurps the individual's free will. Failure to accept responsibility for the decisions we make prevents us from learning, growing, and spiritually maturing in God's Word. In spite of our weaknesses, God's mercy is always available when we go to Him with thankfulness and humility.

SELECTED ATTRIBUTES OF GOD

Now that we have seen what God is not, let us look at some attributes of God. God has different names throughout the Bible.[3] God is *Elohim*, the Creator and *El Shaddai*, our almighty and all powerful God. God is omnipotent, omniscient, and everywhere present. The Lord God is "merciful and gracious, longsuffering, and abundant in goodness and truth" (Exodus 34:6). There are over nine hundred promises in the Bible that document God's blessings to His people.[4]

What follows is a description of some selected attributes of God. This is by no means a definitive list, but illustrates some of the characteristics of our heavenly Father. In highlighting some of God's attributes, His qualities represent the blessings and benefits that come as a result of worshipping the one true God and keeping His commandments. God's heartfelt desire is to bless us with all physical and spiritual blessings. An attitude of gratitude is important in acknowledging God's blessings and recognizing God as our sufficiency in all things.

LOVE

One of the greatest attributes that characterizes God is His love for humanity. The passage, John 3:16–17, exemplifies God's love for His children: "For God so loved the world, that he gave his only begotten Son, that whosoever believeth in him should not perish, but have everlasting life. For God sent not his Son into the world to condemn the world; but that the world through him might be saved."

God's will is that all men and women be saved and come to the knowledge of the truth (1 Timothy 2:4). Paul's epistle to Timothy says that "there is one God, and one mediator between God and men, the man Christ Jesus" (1 Timothy 2:5).

The epistle of John states, "in this was manifested the love of God toward us, because that God sent his only begotten Son into the world, that we might live through him. Herein is love, not that we loved God, but that he loved us, and sent his Son to be the propitiation for our sins" (1 John 4:9–10). *Propitiation* means "full payment for all our sins," because "in due time Christ died for the ungodly" (Romans 5:6).

The Apostle Paul writes in Romans 5:5, "the love of God is shed abroad in our hearts by the Holy Ghost [Spirit] which is given unto us." Furthermore, "God commendeth his love toward us, in that, while we were yet sinners, Christ died for us" (Romans 5:8).

The record of Matthew emphasizes the importance of loving God and others. In an effort to tempt Jesus, a lawyer asked him which was the greatest commandment in the law. Jesus responded by saying that the two great commandments were to "love the Lord thy God with all thy heart, and with all thy soul, and with all thy mind." The second commandment was to "love thy neighbour as thyself" (Matthew 22:37, 39). *Love,* in this context, comes from the Greek word *agapē*. In its deepest and highest sense, this is a spiritual form of love.

The Apostle Paul writes that love is longsuffering, it does not envy, is not "puffed up," is not easily provoked, and "thinketh no evil" (1 Corinthians 13:4, 5). Of faith, hope, and charity *(agapē),* the greatest he writes, is love (1 Corinthians 13:13).

In a world filled with religious, political, social, and economic conflicts, the two greatest commandments of all time, of loving God and loving our neighbors as ourselves, still elude us. In our country, we have the luxury of having the constitutional right of freedom of religion. People can worship God as they choose. However, religious fanaticism exists in any religion. A Christian, with his extreme beliefs, murders a doctor who performs abortions and justifies this heinous act in his mind. A culture performs genital mutilation on young girls and treats women as chattel to justify its religious beliefs. Young people are recruited to perform *jihad* by killing and murdering others in the name of religion. Religious fanaticism, in its myriad forms, must and should be condemned.

When we make a mistake, we can go to God and confess our broken fellowship: "As far as the east is from the west, so far hath he removed our transgressions from us" (Psalm 103:12). Asking God's forgiveness and forgiving yourself and others who have wronged you demonstrates God's love and mercy toward us. When he was dying at Calvary, Jesus prayed, "Father, forgive them; for they know not what they do" (Luke 23:34). This act of forgiveness by Jesus toward his enemies powerfully illustrates his love for all humanity in spite of what was done to him.

PEACE

In a world filled with chaos and confusion, many of us yearn for peace. Peace is not found by focusing on the circumstances and problems of the world. Peace is found when we focus our minds on God's Word. This isn't to say that world leaders shouldn't work toward peace. Romans 12:18 exhorts us, "If it be possible, as much as lieth in you, live peaceably with all men."

We can't always control world events and conflicts among nations. What we can control are our minds and what we choose to think about and dwell on. Isaiah 26:3–4 says, "Thou wilt keep him in perfect peace, whose mind is stayed on thee: because he trusteth in thee. Trust ye in the Lord forever: for in the Lord Jehovah is everlasting strength." David writes in Psalm 29:11, "the Lord will give strength unto his people; the Lord will bless his people with peace."

As the only begotten Son of God, Jesus Christ is the Prince of Peace. In his earthly ministry, he came to reconcile men and women back to God. Those who confess Jesus Christ as Lord and believe that God raised him from the dead are born again and receive the gift of holy spirit: "That if thou shalt confess with thy mouth the Lord Jesus, and shalt believe in thine heart that God hath raised him from the dead, thou shalt be saved. For with the heart man believeth unto righteousness; and with the mouth confession is made unto salvation" (Romans 10:9–10).

Jesus Christ came to restore men and women back to God and to bring wholeness to our lives. He is our advocate and mediator and the means by which we acquire the gift of holy spirit. We don't have to travel to a special building, receive absolution from a holy man, or perform good works to be saved. As long as we confess Jesus Christ as Lord and believe that God raised him from the dead, we receive the gift of holy spirit and eternal life. "For by grace are ye saved through faith; and that not of yourselves: it is the gift of God: Not of works, lest any man should boast" (Ephesians 2:8–9).

For those who choose to believe in him, Jesus said in John 14:27, "Peace I leave with you, my peace I give unto you: not as the world giveth, give I unto you. Let not your heart be troubled, neither let it be afraid." When we focus on the troubles and pressures of the world, we will be emotionally agitated. When we trust in God and focus on and believe the Bible, we will have peace. Jesus taught the following truth: "These things I have spoken unto you, that in me ye might have peace. In the world ye shall have tribulation: but be of good cheer; I have overcome the world" (John 16:33).

The word *tribulation* means "mental pressure." In the world we will experience mental, physical, emotional, and spiritual pressure. When we focus on God and His Word, we will have peace. In spite of the pressures we face, it is possible to have perfect peace as we stay our minds on God and His Word. Just as I need physical food to nourish my body, more importantly, I need spiritual food to nourish my soul. Reading God's Word in the morning prepares me for what lies ahead. Filling my mind with the promises of the Bible prepares me to effectively deal with the pressures of the day. God promises longevity and peace to those who walk according to the standard of His Word: "For length of days, and long life, and peace, shall they add to thee" (Proverbs 3:2).

PROTECTION

The year was 1984, and I was a neophyte in God's Word. I began attending a Christian Bible fellowship on a regular basis. Attending the fellowship whetted my appetite to learn more about the Bible. I was eagerly anticipating a Bible class that I would soon be taking.

One beautiful sunny day in New Jersey, there didn't appear to be a lot of traffic on Route 295 south, a three-lane highway. In the corner of my eye, I noticed a large truck in the right lane, hauling several stacked cars. I was driving in the center lane. Suddenly, something within me said, "Get into the left lane." I began arguing with myself. "Why should I get in the left lane? I'm fine right where I am." However, in the end, I listened to the still, small voice and obeyed and moved to the left lane. No sooner had I changed lanes than the tire on the truck exploded, and the rubber hit the middle lane. I thanked God for that close call. If I stayed in the center lane, I could have been seriously hurt. My immediate thought was that someone or something was trying to prevent me from taking the Bible class. Why? It wasn't until I completed the class that I recognized the spiritual competition I was in. I didn't sign up for the spiritual competition, but by virtue of being born in this world, I was fair game, whether I realized it or not. The Devil did not want me to receive the gift of holy spirit that I learned about in the class, and he certainly did not want me to learn how to manifest the power of God. Acquiring this knowledge enlightened my eyes of spiritual understanding in recognizing and dismantling the Devil's evil works.

We can't always control the attacks by God's archenemy, the Devil. What we can control is our response to those attacks with God's Word. Going to God and asking for His blessings and protection is a spiritual right that we can claim on a daily basis. There is tremendous power in prayer and in operating the gift of holy spirit. We need to learn how to operate the gift of holy spirit and utilize it to bring deliverance to ourselves and others.

I have made it a daily habit to read the Bible in the morning and to pray and thank God for His protection over my life, the lives of my children, my family and loved ones, my country, and even the people I work with.

In studying the Bible, I recognize it is the light of God's Word that manifests the darkness. "Thy word is a lamp unto my feet, and a light unto my path" (Psalm 119:105). The Bible instructs and guides us to avoid the spiritual land mines in the world, "lest Satan should get an advantage of us: for we are not ignorant of his devices" (2 Corinthians 2:11).

Shadrach, Meshach, and Abednego

There are numerous examples throughout the Bible where God protected His people during times of great pressure and distress. In the book of Daniel, chapter three, Nebuchadnezzar, the King of Babylon, proclaimed that at certain times of the day, people had to fall down and worship the golden image he made of himself. If anyone chose not to pay homage to this icon, they would be thrown into a fiery furnace (Daniel 3: 5–6).

The record describes three Judeans, Shadrach, Meshach, and Abednego who chose not to bow down to the golden image. When questioned about their disobedience, the three men's response was, "If it be so, our God whom we serve is able to deliver us from the burning fiery furnace, and he will deliver us out of thine hand, O king" (Daniel 3:17). Furious, Nebuchadnezzar ordered the furnace heated seven times more than normal. The king's men threw Shadrach, Meshach, and Abednego into the fiery furnace. The king's counselors reported seeing four men walking in the midst of the fire (Daniel 3:25). Astounded by this miracle, Nebuchadnezzar ordered the three Judeans out of the fiery furnace. He proclaimed that "every people, nation, and language, which speak any thing amiss against the God of Shadrach, Meshach, and Abednego, shall be cut in pieces, and their houses shall be made a dunghill: because there is no other God that can deliver after this sort" (Daniel 3:29). Nebuchadnezzar then promoted these three men to oversee his affairs in the province of Babylon. This illustration demonstrates that although we may be surrounded by evil, when we cleave to God and hold fast to His promises, we will absolutely receive deliverance and protection in our lives.

Asa

Another example of God's protection illustrates that when a leader seeks and obeys the will of God, God's people are protected. Asa was the third king over the independent state of Judah. The book of 2 Chronicles 14:2–6 records the following:

> Asa did that which was good and right in the eyes of the
> Lord his God:
> For he took away the altars of the strange gods, and the
> high places, and brake down the images, and cut down
> the groves:

And commanded Judah to seek the Lord God of their
fathers, and to do the law and the commandment.
Also he took away out of all the cities of Judah the high
places and the images: and the kingdom was quiet before
him.
And he built fenced cities in Judah: for the land had rest,
and he had no war in those years; because the Lord had
given him rest.

Asa even removed his mother, Maachah, from being queen because she made an idol in a grove. Asa destroyed and burned the idol, and "Asa's heart was perfect with the Lord all his days" (1 Kings 15:14). Azariah's prophecy to Asa was that "the Lord is with you, while ye be with him; and if you seek him, he will be found of you; but if you forsake him, he will forsake you. Be ye strong therefore, and let not your hands be weak: for your work shall be rewarded" (2 Chronicles 15: 2, 7). God is always there when we seek Him and He will never leave us nor forsake us (Hebrews 13:5). "For the Lord shall be thy confidence, and shall keep thy foot from being taken" (Proverbs 3:26).

Christian Missionaries

Another example of God's protection occurred when two Christian missionaries, Dayna Curry and Heather Mercer, were imprisoned by the Taliban in Afghanistan shortly before September 11, 2001. In the face of persecution, their faith never wavered. The women were eventually rescued and brought back to America.[5]

There are numerous examples where people prayed and received deliverance in their lives. Deliverance can occur on a daily basis when we believe that God is a rewarder of those who diligently seek Him (Hebrews 11:6) and that He will protect us in times of need.

FREEDOM

Another attribute of God is that He gives genuine freedom through the accomplishments of Jesus Christ. Jesus Christ came to destroy the spiritual oppression the Devil had over the lives of people. The Bible promises freedom to those who walk according to the standard of His written Word. In Paul's epistle to the Galatians, he writes, "Stand fast therefore in the liberty wherewith Christ hath made us free, and be not entangled again with the yoke of bondage. For in Jesus Christ neither circumcision availeth any thing, nor uncircumcision; but faith which worketh by love. For brethren, ye have been called unto liberty; only use not liberty for an occasion to the flesh, but by love serve one another" (Galatians 5:1, 6, 13).

The Galatians wanted to go back to the Mosaic law and to the traditions and rituals of the past. Paul reproves the Galatians by saying, "O Foolish Galatians, who hath bewitched you, that ye should not obey the truth, before whose eyes Jesus Christ hath been evidently set forth, crucified among you?" (Galatians 3:1). Jesus Christ "redeemed us from the curse of the law" and "if ye be Christ's, then are ye Abraham's seed, and heirs according to the promise" (Galatians 3:13, 29). Genuine freedom comes from having an accurate knowledge and understanding of God's Word.

Jesus Christ came to free people from the mental, physical, emotional, and spiritual bondage they were encased in and to mend, or make whole, the broken pieces of their lives. "If ye continue in my word, then are ye my disciples indeed; And ye shall know the truth, and the truth shall make you free" (John 8:31–32). Continuing in God's Word implies that we remain steadfast and are faithful to God's Word and are not hot one day and cold the next. Applying the principles from the Bible brings ultimate freedom and deliverance in our lives: "Now the Lord is that Spirit: and where the Spirit of the Lord is, there is liberty" (2 Corinthians 3:17).

HEALTH

God's will is that we experience health in all categories of our lives; mental, physical, emotional, and spiritual. The third epistle of John, verse two, says, "Beloved, I wish above all things that thou mayest prosper and be in health, even as thy soul prospereth." The soul represents our thoughts, feelings, emotions, and personality; all those qualities that characterize who we are as individuals.

There is a strong correlation between one's soul life and one's health and prosperity. For example, if I believe that I would be "more spiritual" if I were sick and in poor health, I am not properly aligning my thoughts and actions according to the Word of God. Similarly, if somewhere in my background, I was taught that it is preferable to be poor and to suffer lack, it would be difficult to apply 3 John 2, where God wants me to prosper and be in health. I have a decision to make. Do I believe what someone has erroneously taught me to be true, or do I believe the Word of God? I choose to believe God's Word and not someone else's doctrine. The key to living a more than abundant life is to change our thinking to align with the Word of God. Only then will we experience genuine deliverance in our lives.

There are many examples in my life where people prayed for my health and where I prayed for the health of others, with positive results. A hospital gives its patients a tape to listen to before surgery. On this tape, there are positive affirmations and peaceful music that are designed to relax individuals and raise their level of believing to expect positive results from the surgery. Being fearful and anxious doesn't bode well for the outcome of any surgery. However, with positive believing, God can work in a situation to yield a positive outcome for the patient.[6]

"He sent his word, and healed them, and delivered them from their destructions" (Psalm 107:20). God's Word, when read, properly digested, and applied to your life is like a soothing balm that brings rest to your soul and peace to your mind. "Trust in the Lord with all thine heart; and lean not unto thine own understanding. In all thy ways acknowledge him, and he shall direct thy paths. Be not wise in thine own eyes: fear [respect] the Lord, and depart from evil. It shall be health to thy navel, and marrow to thy bones" (Proverbs 3:5–8).

The Healings of Jesus Christ

Jesus Christ was sent to "heal the brokenhearted" and free people from the spiritual oppression that encased their lives (Luke 4:18). Luke 4:33 records a man possessed with a devil spirit. Jesus demanded that the devil spirit come out of the man, "and when the devil had thrown him in the midst, he came out of him, and hurt him not" (Luke 4:35). Jesus ministered to many people afflicted with diseases and brought deliverance to their lives with the spoken Word (Luke 4:38–41).

The Gospels describe Jesus traveling throughout Galilee, teaching in the synagogues, preaching the gospel of the kingdom of God "and healing all manner of sickness and all manner of disease among the people" (Matthew 4:23).

PROSPERITY

God's will is that we prosper in our lives (3 John 2). David, Solomon, and Abraham are examples of men whom God prospered because of their faithful stand upon God's Word. If God wants prosperity in our lives, why does 1 Timothy 6:10 warn us that "the love of money is the root of all evil: which while some coveted after, they have erred from the faith, and pierced themselves through with many sorrows"? The love of money refers to turning money into an idol or a god. Anything placed above God is a form of idolatry and is considered sin. We seek God first in our lives, and all things shall be *added to,* not subtracted from us (Mathew 6:33). Money in and of itself is not evil. Money acquired through honest means and utilized to help others is a tremendous privilege in stewarding God's abundance.

Tithing

In *Christians Should Be Prosperous,* Victor Paul Wierwille writes, "for a Christian the tithe is a minimum external manifestation of an internal spiritual recognition that God is our basic source of supply and prosperity. In making the tithe our minimum, we share the knowledge of God with others and thus open the floodgates for prosperity to ourselves."[7]

We are reminded that "every good gift and every perfect gift is from above" (James 1:17). When we tithe, or give ten percent of our net income, we acknowledge God as our sufficiency and the giver of all that He has. To be perfectly candid, God does not need the money. Tithing is a reminder to *ourselves* and a recognition of God as the *source* of our sufficiency and blessings. The Apostle Paul reminded the Philippians of this principle when he addressed the topic of giving and receiving. "Not because I desire a gift: but I desire fruit that may abound to your account." "But my God shall supply all your need according to his riches in glory by Christ Jesus" (Philippians 4:17,19).

The tithe is a key principle in the Bible. Abram, whose name was later changed to Abraham, recognized this principle when he gave Melchizedek a "priest of the most high God," tithes of his possessions (Genesis 14:20). The prophet Malachi writes about the blessings that God has for His people who tithe (Malachi 3:10–11).

As we recognize God as our sufficiency, God is able to make all grace abound toward us. Another benefit of tithing is that God protects us from the "devourer" who steals, kills, and destroys. Your attitude, when giving, is also important in receiving God's blessings. "But this I say, He which soweth sparingly shall reap also sparingly; and he which soweth bountifully shall reap also bountifully. Every man according as he purposeth in his heart, so let him give; not grudgingly, or of necessity: for God loveth a cheerful giver. And God is able to make all grace abound toward you; that ye, always having all sufficiency in all things, may abound to every good work" (2 Corinthians 9:6–8).

The law of giving and receiving is an immutable law. Those who practice this law will prosper. All that God asks is that we acknowledge Him by giving a minimum of one tenth of what He has blessed us with. Anything more than one tenth is abundantly sharing God's blessings with others. Practicing the law of tithing and abundant sharing is the greatest job security anyone could have. In the midst of downsizing and layoffs, I have had the privilege of seeing this principle operate in my life.

POWER

One of the reasons I wanted to learn about God and the Bible was because I wanted power in my life. I was tired of being pushed around and being taken advantage of. Growing up, my sister called me "Miss Goody Two Shoes." I was a people pleaser. I wanted to please my parents, my teachers, and the people I worked with.

Being a people pleaser has its drawbacks. There were times when I felt others tried to take advantage of me. Gradually, I learned to become more assertive in my personal and professional life. Early in my professional career, I discovered I had an emotionally abusive boss. Practically everyone in the office was afraid of him. He would belittle and criticize our staff for the smallest mistake. As I began studying God's Word and recognized who I was in Christ, I became spiritually angry with the way he treated his coworkers. I learned to stand up for myself. Armed with the following scriptures, I was able to back down the spiritual attacks that I was experiencing at work.

> *For God hath not given us the spirit of fear; but of power,*
> *and of love, and of a sound mind.*
> 2 Timothy 1:7

> *What shall we then say to these things? If God be for us,*
> *who can be against us?*
> Romans 8:31

If people try to intimidate you or make you feel less than who you are, the following scriptures, when believed and applied, will strengthen your mind to withstand the mental pressures you are experiencing. God can also inspire you to speak in a manner that will defuse a volatile situation. Rather than react with your emotions, you can respond to the situation with the Word of God you have retained in your mind. Here are some scriptures that will strengthen you in this area:

> *A soft answer turneth away wrath: but grievous words stir*
> *up anger.*
> Proverbs 15:1

I can do all things through Christ which strengtheneth me.
Philippians 4:13

Nay, in all these things we are more than conquerors
through him that loved us.
Romans 8:37

Learning and memorizing scriptures will strengthen and provide you with the "spiritual ammunition" you need to focus your thinking on God's Word and not on circumstances. When you make a mistake, as we all do, admit it quickly, apologize, and move on. Many times, a sincere apology goes a long way in defusing a situation. Don't wallow in self-condemnation either, but resolve to do better the next time around: "For if our heart condemn us, God is greater than our heart, and knoweth all things. Beloved, if our heart condemn us not, then have we confidence toward God" (1 John 3:20–21).

In some instances, if your workplace becomes extremely hostile, it might be beneficial to look elsewhere for another job. God will make a way for you to escape and transition to a better position. The important thing is not to fear the situation you are involved in, but have confidence that God is able and willing to bless you with a comparable or better position in your career.

Jesus Christ's Ministry

The Scriptures, when believed and acted upon, have power to positively influence our personal lives and transform the lives of others. This same power is demonstrated through the public ministry of Jesus Christ. There are numerous records in the Gospels where Jesus healed the sick, raised people from the dead, and preached the kingdom of God (Matthew 9:35). In Luke 8:27, Jesus met a man possessed with devil spirits. When the man saw Jesus approaching, he fell down and said with a loud voice, "What have I to do with thee, Jesus, thou Son of God most high? I beseech thee, torment me not" (Luke 8:28). Jesus calmly asked him his name and the answer was, "Legion because many devils were entered into him" (Luke 8:30). Jesus cast the devil spirits out of the man, and the devil spirits entered into a herd of swine feeding on the mountain; the herd ran violently down a steep place into the lake and drowned.

God's power is further demonstrated in the record of Luke where Jesus appointed seventy disciples and sent them to preach the kingdom of God. "The harvest truly is great, but the labourers are few: pray ye therefore the Lord of the harvest, that he would send forth labourers into his harvest" (Luke 10:2). When the seventy returned with great joy they reported back saying, "Lord even the devils are subject unto us through thy name. And he said unto them, I beheld Satan as lightning fall from heaven. Behold, I give unto you power to tread on serpents and scorpions, and over all the power of the enemy: and nothing shall by any means hurt you. Notwithstanding in this rejoice not, that the spirits are subject unto you; but rather rejoice, because your names are written in heaven" (Luke 10:17–20).

Jesus performed many other miracles manifesting God's power. He was able to perform these miracles because he received the spirit of God upon him without measure (John 3:34).

With love, compassion, and forgiveness, Jesus demonstrated God's power and merciful love to others. Jesus knew that in order for people to receive the same power from God, the gift of holy spirit, he would have to depart.

But the Comforter, which is the Holy Ghost [Spirit], whom the Father will send in my name, he shall teach you all things, and bring all things to your remembrance, whatsoever I have said unto you.
John 14:26

Nevertheless I tell you the truth; It is expedient for you that I go away; for if I go not away, the Comforter will not come unto you; but if I depart, I will send him unto you.
John 16:7

Verily, verily, I say unto you, He that believeth on me, the works that I do shall he do also; and greater works than these shall he do; because I go unto my Father.
John 14:12

In chapter six, we will see how the Christians in the first-century church were able to walk with this same power of God as a result of manifesting the gift of holy spirit received on the day of Pentecost.

PRACTICAL KEYS TO
APPLYING THE BIBLE

1. Praise and thankfulness are two keys to effective prayer. There are over nine hundred promises in the Bible. Find the promises that you want to claim in the Bible, thank God, and take the believing action steps for God to bring them to pass in your life.

2. Start a prayer journal and write down your personal and spiritual goals. As you achieve your current goals, set new goals for your life.

3. Document and date all the blessings that God has performed in your life.

4. Find a prayer partner to pray with, and believe together as you claim the promises in the Bible.

5. Look up the scriptures in this chapter and begin applying them in your life.

6. Research the following scriptures for further study and application.

SCRIPTURES FOR FURTHER STUDY

Psalm 1:1–3
Psalm 35:27
Psalm 147:1–7

Matthew 18:19
Mark 9:23
Mark 11:24
Luke 4:18–21
Luke 8:50
1 John 5:14–15

CHAPTER FOUR

THE SPIRITUAL COMPETITION

For we wrestle not against flesh and blood, but against principalities, against powers, against the rulers of the darkness of this world, against spiritual wickedness in high places.
Ephesians 6:12

It was a cold, bitter winter evening. I was driving home late at night after teaching an off-campus graduate class in Paterson, New Jersey. Unfamiliar with the roads, I had a sickening feeling that I was lost. I pulled over to the side of the highway to check my written directions. I could barely see, except for the dim overhead light in my Dodge Caravan. As I struggled to read my directions, suddenly I heard a shot and the sound of glass shattering in my back window. I quickly started the car and prayed to God to help me find my way back to civilization. Unexpectedly, I saw a light and started driving toward a gas station and discovered the main road. Apparently I had somehow veered off.

When I pulled in to the gas station and parked my car, I surveyed my shattered rear window and discovered a sixteen-inch crossbow arrow on the back seat. Distraught at seeing the damage, my first thought was, "Damn, now I'm going to have to pay for this." My second thought was, "Thank God the shooter didn't aim for my head." Perhaps he did, and God protected me. I could have been killed. Shaken, I called the police and reported the incident.

The next week I had a decision to make. Should I continue teaching the course or just quit? Growing in God's Word, I recognized the incident as a spiritual attack and decided the only way I was going to conquer my fear was to confront the very thing that I feared. Armed with Philippians 4:13 and 2 Timothy 1:7 and a better set of directions, I went back to Paterson, taught the course, and navigated my way home safely till the end of the semester.

I use this personal incident to illustrate the fact that the Devil attacks without provocation. Evil is real. "Be sober, be vigilant; because your adversary the devil, as a roaring lion, walketh about, seeking whom he may devour" (1 Peter 5:8). Evil is manifested when people, by their own free will and a hardness of heart to the written Word, allow their minds to be influenced by devil spirits and serve as conduits to steal, kill, and destroy. The Devil is a parasite who feeds on people's fears and weaknesses.

"The greatest trick the devil ever pulled was convincing the world that he doesn't exist," says Keyser Soze in the film, *The Usual Suspects*.[1] According to a 2009 scientific poll sponsored by the Barna Group, a Christian research company, four out of ten Christians (40 percent) agreed that Satan "is not a living being but is a symbol of evil."[2] Andrew Delbanco writes, "So the work of the devil is everywhere, but no one knows where to find him. We live in the most brutal century in human history, but instead of stepping forward to take the credit, he has rendered himself invisible."[3]

Because the Devil is a spirit who disguises himself as the "angel of light" (2 Corinthians 11:14) and who is the "prince of this world" (John 14:30), he is invisible to the naked eye. His works are manifested in the senses realm through suffering, poverty, murder, death, and destructive evil. He is the great counterfeiter, liar, pretender, and parasite who feeds off of good in order to obstruct the purposes of the one true God. His bloody tracks are left in the horrific murder of innocent children and adults at Sandy Hook Elementary School in Newtown, Connecticut, in a movie theater in Aurora, Colorado, at Virginia Tech University in Blacksburg, Virginia, at the Boston Marathon bombings, at the Washington Navy Yard mass shooting—and the list goes on. Whenever we witness the senseless murder of innocent children and adults, the Devil and his spirit kingdom, that is, devil spirits, have worked through the minds of people who carried out their murderous acts.

THE SPIRITUAL COMPETITION
Two Gods
The Bible states there are two gods. God, the Father of our Lord and Savior Jesus Christ, and the Devil, the god of this world: "In whom the god of this world hath blinded the minds of them which believe not, lest the light of the glorious gospel of Christ, who is the image of God, should shine unto them" (2 Corinthians 4:4).

Prior to his public ministry, Jesus Christ was taken into the wilderness and tempted by the Devil for forty days and forty nights. In Matthew 4:8–9, the Devil took Jesus up into a high mountain and showed him all the kingdoms of the world and told him, "All these things will I give thee, if thou wilt fall down and worship me."[4] Jesus's response to this spiritual attack was, "Get thee hence, Satan: for it is written, Thou shalt worship the Lord thy God, and him only shalt thou serve" (Matthew 4:10).

Jesus Christ was not interested in acquiring worldly power or riches. He came to preach the gospel of the kingdom of God to the lost sheep of the house of Israel and to heal all manner of sickness and diseases (Matthew 4:23).[5] When he began his public ministry, "the people which sat in darkness saw great light; and to them which sat in the region and shadow of death light is sprung up" (Matthew 4:16). The purpose of Jesus Christ's ministry was to reconcile people back to God and to destroy the works of the Devil. "He that committeth sin is of the devil; for the devil sinneth from the beginning. For this purpose the Son of God was manifested, that he might destroy the works of the devil" (1 John 3:8).

Up until the birth of Jesus Christ, people were in spiritual darkness, blinded and in bondage to the Devil and without hope in this world: "For all have sinned, and come short of the glory of God; Being justified freely by his grace through the redemption that is in Christ Jesus: Whom God hath set forth to be a propitiation through faith in his blood, to declare his righteousness for the remission of sins that are past, through the forbearance of God… Therefore we conclude that a man is justified by faith [believing] without the deeds of the law" (Romans 3:23–25, 28).

The Devil is an equal opportunity destroyer who steals, kills, and destroys (John 10:10). As the epitome of evil, he works through the lives of people, culture, and the environment to terrorize and distract individuals from the light of the one true God. As the author of death (Hebrews 2:14), the Devil would kill his own children if he thought it would advance his purposes.

Throughout the Bible, this spirit being is referred to as Satan (Mark 1:13), Lucifer (Isaiah 14:12), Beelzebub (Matthew 12:24), the Devil (Matthew 4:1), the tempter (Matthew 4:3), the god of this world (2 Corinthians 4:4), a murderer and liar (John 8:44), the prince of this world (John 14:30), the devourer (Malachi 3:11), the destroyer (1 Corinthians 10:10), the adversary (1 Peter 5:8), the dragon, serpent, and deceiver (Revelation 12:9), the prince of the power of the air (Ephesians 2:2), and the accuser of the brethren (Revelation 12:10). Through a proper understanding of the Word of God, we can distinguish between the genuine and the counterfeit. The light of God's Word exposes the darkness of this world. The Bible is the critical filter that separates truth from error. The power of the written Word, the gift of holy spirit, and believing overcome the devil spirit world through the accomplished works of Jesus Christ.

The Devil Spirit World

The Bible says, "Be sober, be vigilant; because your adversary the devil, as a roaring lion, walketh about, seeking whom he may devour" (1 Peter 5:8). God wants us to be knowledgeable about His written Word, which is a blueprint and a guide for life, "lest Satan should get an advantage of us: for we are not ignorant of his devices" (2 Corinthians 2:11).

The Fall

The prophet Isaiah describes the fall of Lucifer. Ironically, the meaning of the Latin word, "Lucifer," is "light-bearer." Lucifer was once the angel of light, second in command to God. As a result of pride and egotism, Lucifer wasn't satisfied with being second in command. He wanted to be God: "How art thou fallen from heaven, O Lucifer, son of the morning! how art thou cut down to the ground, which didst weaken the nations! For thou hast said in thine heart, I will ascend into heaven, I will exalt my throne above the stars of God: I will sit also upon the mount of the congregation, in the sides of the north: I will ascend above the heights of the clouds; I will be like the most High" (Isaiah 14:12–14).

Proverbs 16:18 states, "pride goeth before destruction, and an haughty spirit before a fall." As a result of Lucifer's rebellion, he and one-third of the angels were cast down from heaven and "made the world as a wilderness and destroyed the cities thereof" (Isaiah 14:17). The book of Revelation describes the spiritual warfare that took place in heaven:

> *And there was war in heaven: Michael and his angels fought against the dragon; and the dragon fought and his angels, And prevailed not; neither was their place found any more in heaven.*
>
> *And the great dragon was cast out, that old serpent, called the Devil, and Satan, which deceiveth the whole world: he was cast out into the earth, his angels were cast out with him.*
>
> *And I heard a loud voice saying in heaven, Now is come salvation, and strength, and the kingdom of our God, and the power of his Christ: for the accuser of our brethren is cast down, which accused them before our God day and night.*
>
> *And they overcame him by the blood of the Lamb, and by the word of their testimony; and they loved not their lives unto the death.*
>
> *Therefore rejoice, ye heavens, and ye that dwell in them. Woe to the inhabiters of the earth and of the sea! for the devil is come down unto you, having great wrath, because he knoweth that he hath but a short time.*
>
> Revelation 12:7–12

*And they worshipped the dragon which gave power unto
the beast: and they worshipped the beast, saying, Who is
like unto the beast? who is able to make war with him?*
Revelation 13:4

Revelation 12:13 warns us that when the dragon was cast
into the earth, he "persecuted the woman which brought forth
the man child." Who is the "man child?" The "man child" refers to the birth of Jesus Christ. To this day, the Devil continues
"to make war with the remnant of her seed, which keep the
commandments of God, and have the testimony of Jesus Christ"
(Revelation 12:17).

Since the fall of Adam, the evil forces of the wicked one continue to attack, persecute, and seek to destroy those who keep
the commandments of the one true God and who bear witness of
the Lord Jesus Christ. Through the "blood of the Lamb," Jesus
Christ, we are able to claim the victory over the devil spirit realm.

*For whatsoever is born of God overcometh the world: and
this is the victory that overcometh the world, even our
faith [believing].*
*Who is he that overcometh the world, but he that believeth
that Jesus is the Son of God?*
1 John 5:4–5

*But thanks be to God, which giveth us the victory
through our Lord Jesus Christ.*
1 Corinthians 15:57

Since the beginning of time, the Devil's insatiable desire was to
be God. If he is unable to garner worship directly, through systemat-

ic error, he seduces people into worshiping icons and false doctrines. Deceived by the spirit of error, people are led down a path of confusion and ultimate destruction. Pressure or pleasure are the means by which he seduces and beguiles people to turn away from the one true God and ultimately from the Word of God. Understanding and applying scriptures from the Bible, and operating the gift of holy spirit, expose his devices and the true nature of his deception.

LIGHT AND DARKNESS

God, through His written Word and His only begotten Son Jesus Christ, represents light. In contrast, the Devil, as the incarnation of evil, represents darkness.

The contrast between light and darkness is described in the following passage: "Light is come into the world, and men loved darkness rather than light, because their deeds were evil. For every one that doeth evil hateth the light, neither cometh to the light, lest his deeds should be reproved. But he that doeth truth cometh to the light, that his deeds may be manifest, that they are wrought in God" (John 3:19–21).

Rebellion against the light is described in the book of Job. Job states, "they are of those that rebel against the light; they know not the ways thereof, nor abide in the paths thereof" (Job 24:13).

SELECTED ATTRIBUTES OF THE DEVIL

As the one true God represents love, peace, protection, freedom, health, prosperity, and power, the Devil represents the antithesis of all that is holy, good, and perfect. It is not within the scope of this book to describe all the attributes of the Devil. However, we will identify some of his characteristics that are described in the Word of God.

SEDUCER

One strategy Satan uses to deceive us is to appeal to our emotions and carnal instincts. Ecclesiastes 1:9 says, "there is no new thing under the sun." Today, as in the past, men and women are seduced by the "lust of the flesh, and the lust of the eyes, and the pride of life" (1 John 2:16).

Contemporary life is filled with examples of powerful men who allowed themselves to be seduced by women outside of their marriages. Egotism, and the belief that they are somehow above the law and therefore above a universal moral standard, primes them for their eventual downfall. Whether it is through a prostitute, a mistress, or the use of an escort service, promising careers have been toppled because of a defect in moral character and judgment. With every decision, there are always consequences.

The Devil knows what our weaknesses are. He has studied us since the day we were born. The Devil is a master at manipulating human behavior. Fully cognizant of our weaknesses, he draws people away from the standard of God's Word and tries to seduce us with the temptations of the world.

The importance of turning our weaknesses into strengths with God's Word, prayer, and hard work is critical if we are to effectively deal with the Devil's spiritual, mental, physical, and emotional attacks. Unless we eliminate our weaknesses, it is just a matter of time before the Devil sets up the right conditions that will ultimately bring about our downfall. Succumbing to the works of the flesh, without any moral restraint, ultimately leads to spiritual destruction.

Seduction is not only confined to illicit sexual encounters. Seduction can also take the form of philosophies and doctrines that are contrary to the Word of God.

Paul's epistle to the Galatians warns them of the "works of the flesh," when he says, "Now the works of the flesh are manifest, which are these; Adultery fornication, uncleanness, lasciviousness, Idolatry, witchcraft, hatred, variance, emulations, wrath, strife, seditions, heresies, Envyings, murders, drunkenness, revelings, and such like: of the which I tell you before, as I have also told you in time past, that they which do such things shall not inherit the kingdom of God" (Galatians 5:19–21).

First Timothy 4:1–2 warns us, "now the Spirit speaketh expressly, that in the latter times some shall depart from the faith, giving heed to seducing spirits, and doctrines of devils; speaking lies in hypocrisy; having their conscience seared with a hot iron." Second Timothy 3:13 says, "evil men and seducers shall wax worse and worse, deceiving, and being deceived."

The Bible describes how false Christs and false prophets will rise up and will demonstrate "signs and wonders, to seduce...even the elect" (Mark 13:22). Through the kingdoms of the world and "doctrines of devils," the adversary seduces and leads people away from the one true God and the Word of God.

Without an accurate understanding of God's Word, it is easy to be seduced with doctrines that are contrary to the Bible. Isaiah 5:13 says, "My people are gone into captivity, because they have no knowledge." Hosea 4:6 declares, "My people are destroyed for lack of knowledge." What knowledge are they referring to? It's the knowledge of the Word of God. God's people are mentally, emotionally, physically, and spiritually destitute because they lack an accurate knowledge of the Bible. The prophet Isaiah warns us of the consequences of spiritual error: "Woe unto them that call evil good, and good evil; that put darkness for light, and light for darkness; that put bitter for sweet, and sweet for bitter" (Isaiah 5:20).

Without an accurate knowledge and understanding of the Bible, people are confused about the distinction between good and evil. They call good evil and evil good. Psalm 82:5 states, "They know not, neither will they understand; they walk on in darkness: all the foundations of the earth are out of course." Furthermore, "they will not frame their doings to turn unto their God: for the spirit of whoredoms is in the midst of them, and they have not known the Lord" (Hosea 5:4).

PERVERSE

When the children of Israel turned away from worshipping the one true God, they became a "perverse and crooked generation" (Deuteronomy 32:5). Through the worship of "strange gods" and idols, they committed abominable works. "They sacrificed unto devils, not to God; to gods whom they knew not, to new gods that came newly up, whom your fathers feared not. Of the Rock that begat thee thou art unmindful, and hast forgotten God that formed thee" (Deuteronomy 32:17–18).

In addition to idolatry, perversion can be seen in the form of child abuse, child pornography, pedophilia, human trafficking, rape, bestiality, and inhumane acts that are repulsive to the sensibilities of any moral code of conduct or ethics. Those who commit such heinous acts against humanity have opened their minds to devil spirit influence. Their minds are like cottage cheese. They have freely opened their minds to devil spirits who cannibalize all remnants of sound, moral, and rational thinking. Proverbs 4:16 describe those who are unable to sleep unless they commit evil; "for they sleep not, except they have done mischief [evil]; and their sleep is taken away, unless they cause some to fall."

MURDERER

Psalm 37:32 warns us, "the wicked watcheth the righteous and seeketh to slay him." Throughout the Bible, there are many examples of individuals who commit murder. One example of murder is the mistaken belief that human sacrifice is necessary to worship God. The Israelites were surrounded by cultures that practiced human sacrifice.[6] The Bible is clear that human sacrifice is contrary to worshipping the one true God: "And they served their idols: which were a snare unto them. Yea, they sacrificed their sons and their daughters unto devils, and shed innocent blood, even the blood of their sons and of their daughters, whom they sacrificed unto the idols of Canaan: and the land was polluted with blood. Thus were they defiled with their own works, and went a whoring with their own inventions" (Psalm 106:36–39).

Other examples of murder were when Cain slew his brother Abel (Genesis 4:8) and when Herod murdered all the children in Bethlehem, and in the surrounding area, who were two years of age and under (Matthew 2:16).

During his public ministry, Jesus Christ confronted the Pharisees, the religious leaders of the day, when they boasted they were of Abraham's seed but were secretly planning to kill Jesus (John 8:37). He said, "Ye are of your father the devil, and the lusts of your father ye will do. He was a murderer from the beginning, and abode not in the truth, because there is no truth in him. When he speaketh a lie, he speaketh of his own: for he is a liar, and the father of it" (John 8:44).

The ultimate murder of an innocent man occurred when the religious leaders had Jesus crucified. In spite of the murder of Jesus Christ, God was able to raise him from the dead. Through the accomplished works of Jesus Christ, those who confess him as Lord and believe that God raised him from the dead can manifest power from on high and have eternal life (Romans 10:9–10).

Other examples of devilish works include the mass murder of millions of Jews during the Holocaust and the grotesque rituals of the Satanic church.[7] Moreover, the shedding of innocent blood on September 11, 2001, and the murder of innocent children and adults at Sandy Hook Elementary School in Newtown, Connecticut, are events that will be forever imprinted in our national consciousness. For those who mistakenly believe they are doing God's will by committing murder, Jesus Christ prophetically stated, "Yea, the time cometh, that whosoever killeth you will think that he doeth God service. And these things will they do unto you, because they have not known the Father, nor me" (John 16:2–3).

John 16:2–3 clearly says those who commit murder, and believe they are doing God's will, do not know the one true God nor do they know our Lord and Savior Jesus Christ.

SICKNESS

It is the Devil's nature to steal, kill, and destroy (John 10:10). His goal is to break us down mentally, physically, emotionally, and spiritually. Sickness can never come from the one true God, nor is it ever an attempt to "test" or "tempt" an individual to become more spiritual. I know when I become sick, it is invariably because of stress, not getting enough rest, and not eating properly. Sickness is never a blessing from God, as it prevents us from living lives that are more than abundant, which God has called us to do (3 John 2). The Devil's goal is to break us down mentally, physically, and emotionally and afflict us with disease and ultimately death.

PRIDE

"Pride goeth before destruction, and an haughty spirit before a fall. Better it is to be of an humble spirit with the lowly, than to divide the spoil with the proud" (Proverbs 16:18–19). Pride and egotism caused Lucifer's downfall, and it is pride and egotism that ultimately leads to an individual's demise. "Every one that is proud in heart is an abomination to the Lord" (Proverbs 16:5).

By working through and influencing the environment, culture, and our five senses, the adversary continues to oppress and control the lives of people. "The wicked in his pride doth persecute the poor" (Psalm 10:2).

The entanglements of the world are numerous. Debt, child abuse, alcoholism, spousal abuse, drugs, rampant sexuality, adultery, and witchcraft are some of the snares of the world. Seeing with spiritual eyes requires spiritual discernment: "But the natural man receiveth not the things of the Spirit of God: for they are foolishness unto him: neither can he know them, because they are spiritually discerned" (1 Corinthians 2:14).

Jesus Christ had God's spirit upon him without measure (John 3:34). He was able to spiritually discern the hypocrisy of the religious leaders when they criticized his disciples for eating bread with unwashed hands (Mark 7:2). He confronted the Pharisees and scribes and accused them of following the traditions of men and not the commandments of God.

Jesus taught his disciples, that those things which come from within defile the person: "For from within, out of the heart of men, proceed evil thoughts, adulteries, fornications, murders, Thefts, covetousness, wickedness, deceit, lasciviousness, an evil eye, blasphemy, pride, foolishness: All these evil things come from within, and defile the man" (Mark 7:21–23).

ACCUSER

Revelation 12:10 refers to the Devil as the "accuser of the brethren." Just as the Devil tried to get Jesus to doubt that he was the Son of God, in Matthew 4, the Devil continually tries to get Christians to question their sonship rights as born-again believers.[8]

Through the words and actions of people, the Devil has tried to attack me with feelings of inadequacy, guilt, fear, threats, and intimidation. As a result of growing in my understanding of the Bible, I began to recognize the source of these spiritual attacks. Empowered by the gift of holy spirit, I learned the importance of walking by the spirit and avoiding people and situations that would place me or my loved ones in harm's way. It is important to consistently pray for those we love and believe that God will protect them from harm.

Mark 3:1–4 describes the record of Jesus entering the synagogue and meeting a man with a withered hand. The religious leaders watched Jesus to see whether or not he would heal the man on the Sabbath day, so they might accuse him of breaking the law. Jesus asked the man with the withered hand to come forward. "And he saith unto them Is it lawful to do good on the sabbath days, or to do evil? To save life, or to kill? But they held their peace. And when he had looked round about on them with anger, being grieved for the hardness of their hearts, he saith unto the man, Stretch forth thine hand. And he stretched it out: and his hand was restored whole as the other" (Mark 3:4–5).

Immediately, the Pharisees consulted with the Herodians to see how they might murder Jesus. Jealousy, envy, and hatred for the Son of God caused the adversary to work through the religious leaders who accused Jesus of being possessed with a devil spirit. "He hath Beelzebub, and by the prince of the devils casteth he out devils" (Mark 3:22). Jesus confronted them by asking, "How can Satan cast out Satan? And if a kingdom be divided against itself, that kingdom cannot stand. And if a house be divided against itself, that house cannot stand. And if Satan rise up against himself, and be divided, he cannot stand, but hath an end" (Mark: 3:23–26). With precise logic, Jesus confronted his accusers with God's Word.

By working in the lives of people, the Devil continues to accuse those who worship the one true God. If the Devil is unable to destroy the Word of God, he seeks to draw us away from learning the Bible. With the birth, life, death, resurrection, and ascension of Jesus Christ, the Devil is already defeated. When we retain the Word of God in our minds, operate the gift of holy spirit, and speak and share God's Word with boldness, we are destroying the works of the Devil (John 14:12, 1 John 3:8).

DESTROYER

When I think of the September 11 attacks on the World Trade Center and the senseless massacre of innocent children and adults in Newtown, Connecticut I think of the destroyer.[9]

David writes in Psalm 37:35, "I have seen the wicked in great power, and spreading himself like a green bay tree." We need only survey the events of the world to recognize the evil destruction of God's archenemy, the Devil. "So I returned, and considered all the oppressions that are done under the sun: and behold the tears of such as were oppressed, and they had no comforter; and on the side of their oppressors there was power; but they had no comforter" (Ecclesiastes 4:1).

Prior to the birth of Jesus Christ and the gift of holy spirit given on the day of Pentecost, there was no comforter and no genuine power to counteract the Devil's destructive evil. Jesus Christ served as humanity's redeemer to save us from this destructive evil.

Paul's epistle to the Philippians is a warning to those who walk contrary to the Word of God: "Brethren, be followers together of me, and mark them which walk so as ye have us for an ensample. For many walk, of whom I have told you often, and now tell you even weeping, that they are the enemies of the cross of Christ: Whose end is destruction, whose God is their belly, and whose glory is in their shame, who mind earthly things" (Philippians 3:17–19).

In spite of the destructive evil we observe in the world, "Great is our Lord, and of great power: his understanding is infinite. The Lord lifteth up the meek: he casteth the wicked down to the ground" (Psalm 147:5–6). Those who humble themselves before God and align their lives with the standard of God's Word will receive God's protection from the Devil's destructive evil.

> *The fear of man bringeth a snare: but whoso putteth his trust in the Lord shall be safe.*
> Proverbs 29:25

> *And they that know thy name will put their trust in thee: for thou, Lord, hast not forsaken them that seek thee.*
> Psalm 9:10

> *I have been young, and now am old; yet have I not seen the righteous forsaken, nor his seed begging bread.*
> Psalm 37:25

When Jesus Christ was raised from the dead, he "spoiled principalities and powers" and "made a shew of them openly, triumphing over them in it" (Colossians 2:15). He also "led captivity captive, and gave gifts unto men" (Ephesians 4:8). As born-again believers, we are reminded, "Ye are of God, little children, and have overcome them: because greater is he that is in you, than he that is in the world" (1 John 4:4).

PRACTICAL KEYS TO APPLYING THE BIBLE

1. Develop a list of things you would like to pray for including yourself, your family, your friends, your job, your community, your country, and the world.

2. With an attitude of gratitude, pray daily with your prayer partner for the blessings you want to see come to pass in your life, and in the lives of others, according to God's Word.

3. Teach your children how to apply biblical principles in their lives and document the results.

4. Start attending a Bible fellowship in your area.

5. Continue reading the Bible faithfully.

6. Apply the biblical principles you are learning from God's Word, such as tithing, and document God's blessings in your life.

7. Review the scriptures in this chapter for further study, and write them down on index cards. Refer to the scriptures when you are challenged in your mind with thoughts that are contrary to God's Word.

8. Continue to enroll in Bible classes that teach you how to understand and apply biblical scriptures in your life.

SCRIPTURES FOR FURTHER STUDY

Deuteronomy 4:9–10

Deuteronomy 6:7

Joshua 1:9

Isaiah 8:12

Isaiah 26:3–4

Psalm 28:7

2 Timothy 1:7

2 Corinthians 9:8

2 Corinthians 10:5

Ephesians 6:1–4

CHAPTER FIVE

SENSE KNOWLEDGE VERSUS SPIRITUAL KNOWLEDGE

Now we have received, not the spirit of the world, but the spirit which is of God; that we might know the things that are freely given to us of God.
1 Corinthians 2:12

PRAYING FOR A MIRACLE

"Oh no!" I stared at my computer screen. I couldn't believe my eyes. Within a short period of time, the value of my retirement fund had plummeted to a loss of over one hundred thousand dollars, and there was no end in sight. I wanted to stop the hemorrhaging, but there was nothing I could do. To make matters worse, in a series of cost-cutting measures, the governor of our state cut our university program's budget by $1.2 million. The employees in my department had three options: 1) Look for another job, 2) Voluntarily retire, or 3) Be laid off. The options weren't pretty. What was once a healthy and thriving department at a world-class research institution dwindled to a handful of individuals.

I decided not to panic and instead believed God would meet my need for another position, preferably at the same university. As far as the stock market was concerned, I couldn't put my trust in uncertain riches. "God is my sufficiency," I reasoned, "not the stock market." In time, I believed the stock market would bounce back as it has in the past. In the meantime, I needed a job. People were being laid off and unemployment was rising. God would see me through this challenging period of my life. God always came through in the nick of time.

I decided to believe Philippians 4:19: "But my God shall supply all your need according to his riches in glory by Christ Jesus." How wealthy is God? God who created the heavens and the earth could surely provide me with another job. Is there anything too hard for God (Jeremiah 32:27)? Or as Romans 8:31 says, "If God be for us who can be against us?" I ran these and a number of other scriptures through my mind. I also reached out to my Bible fellowship and other faithful believers to inform them about my need, so they could pray and believe with me for another job.

There are four major things I have learned as a result of studying the Bible: 1) There is power in prayer, 2) There is power in believing the Word of God, 3) There is power in acting on the Word of God, and 4) God's Word works! Whether it is a new job, a health situation, a financial challenge, marital infidelity, or any other problem, God is always there when we turn to Him for guidance and answers in life.

To stay my mind on the promises of God, I wrote several scriptures down on index cards and taped them on my kitchen cabinet, my bedroom dresser, and my bathroom mirror. Some of the scriptures I wrote were 2 Timothy 1:7, 2 Corinthians 10:5, Proverbs 3:5–6, and Joshua 1:9. In addition to reading the Bible in the morning, wherever I turned in my home, the Word of God was right there to remind me that God would bring to pass His deliverance in my life.

There is tremendous power in having a group of individuals believe and pray with you. Matthew 18:19 says that "if two of you shall agree on earth as touching anything that they shall ask, it shall be done for them of my Father which is in heaven." Surrounded by positive believing and prayers strengthened my resolve to find another position within the university.

Answered prayer comes not in the form of wishing things would happen. Answered prayer occurs when we take the believing action to make things happen according to His written Word. In addition to taking the necessary steps to raise my believing with God's Word, I knocked on doors, searched the Internet for job postings, submitted my application and résumé, and followed up with numerous phone calls. God expects us to do everything we can with our five senses, and He will do His part in meeting our need. God works when we take the believing action to appropriate His blessings.

One of the greatest challenges in learning to walk by the Word of God, and the renewed mind, is to believe the promises in God's Word in spite of being surrounded by negative circumstances. Newspaper headlines proclaimed that we were in a deep recession, unemployment was rising, the housing market was crumbling, and people were losing faith in the economy. America's financial system was fraught with scandal, greed, and corruption. I decided not to believe the newspaper headlines and the television media. God was my sufficiency, and he would help me find the ideal job. I continued to think and confess this in my mind. In the midst of this challenging time, I continued to abundantly share of my net income.[1] "Prove me now herewith, saith the Lord of hosts, if I will not open you the windows of heaven, and pour you out a blessing, that there shall not be room enough to receive it" (Malachi 3:10). Biblical principles work and are not contingent upon peoples' opinions or worldly circumstances.

I applied for many positions at the university. Positions I thought would be a good match, given my experience and educational background, were not offered. I often heard the expression, "You are overqualified." Faced with rejection and unreturned phone calls, I prayed to God to show me where He wanted me to be. Tired of looking at jobs through my five senses, I sought God's wisdom and guidance in leading me to a job that would be a blessing to me as well as to the people for whom I would work.

Effective prayer requires having an attitude of gratitude. Thanking God for the blessings I already had opened the door to receiving additional blessings from God. I learned not to be anxious about anything: "Be careful for nothing; but in every thing by prayer and supplication with thanksgiving let your requests be made known unto God" (Philippians 4:6). God is never late. His timing is always perfect. As I am faithful to God, God is faithful to His Word.

In the nick of time, a position I applied for opened up. I was able to transfer to an excellent position at the university. My new job was perfect. Based on my experience and educational background, I even received a promotion and a raise! "Now unto him that is able to do exceedingly abundantly above all that we ask or think, according to the power that worketh in us"—it was definitely an Ephesians 3:20 victory! I wanted to shout my deliverance from the rooftops. As a result of this victory and many others, I continue to share what God has done for me. He will do no less for you as you believe and apply His Word. "If thou faint in the day of adversity, thy strength is small," Proverbs 24:10 declares.

I learned not to faint in adversity but to endure and prevail until God's victory came to pass.

THE CAVE

In Book VII of the *Republic*,[2] Plato describes the allegory of the cave. During their entire lifetime, people lived in the cave, imprisoned in darkness. Their necks and legs were shackled in chains. A crackling fire in back of the cave provided the only source of light. Visible to the naked eye were the shadows of their bodies that were reflected on the wall in front of them. To the prisoners, the shadows on the cave represented reality.

When the prisoners were released from the cave and walked into the sunlight, they recognized another reality distinct from their previous experience. The images in the cave represented the world of appearances. This was a world of image-making or imagination, belief, opinion, and perception. The world of the senses represented one dimension of reality, but it was limited in scope and possibilities.

Plato used this allegory to illustrate the importance of education and the "journey of the soul to the intelligible realm." In his ideal republic, Plato advocated a course of study, such as mathematics, to understand the various forms of knowledge leading to the highest form or the "Form of the Good." Education, for Plato, involved "turning a soul from a kind of day that is night to the true day, being the upward way to reality which we say is true philosophy."[3] In his ideal educational system, Plato described the intelligible world as a world where reasoning, thinking, understanding, and rational intuition were important intellectual qualities to acquire.

In many ways, we are like the people living in a cave. Plato accurately made the distinction between the world of appearances and the world of ideas and rational thinking. Many people eat, sleep, wake up, and pursue their routine existences without thinking. As one character in a popular movie asked, "Is this all there is?" Philosophy is a world of ideas. Ideas have no boundaries or limitations. If it can be conceived, then it's only a matter of time before an idea will be transformed into its concrete form. All great inventions and discoveries began with an idea.

LIMITATIONS OF PHILOSOPHY

As important as philosophy is to intellectual thought and discussion, it is limited in acquiring true wisdom. Asking the right question does not necessarily imply arriving at a correct answer. In its purest form, the pursuit of philosophy leads to further questions. Pilate's question to Jesus Christ, "What is truth?" in John 18:38, is a question many people still ask today and whose answer continually eludes them.

Colin McGinn, in his autobiography, *The Making of a Philosopher,* describes philosophical discussion as a kind of "intellectual blood sport, in which egos get bruised and buckled, even impaled." Clearly, philosophical discussion and debate are not for the fainthearted. McGinn writes, "In fact, truth to tell, philosophy and ego are never very far apart…I have seen people white and dry-mouthed before giving a talk to a tough-minded audience, and visibly shaken afterward. No one likes to be publicly refuted, and in philosophy it happens all the time. In Evans I saw someone with considerable debating skills, and I was no doubt attracted to the kind of power and respect that goes with that. Plain showing off is also a feature of philosophical life."[4]

Colossians 2:8 warns us to beware of "philosophy and vain deceit, after the tradition of men, after the rudiments of the world, and not after Christ." In Paul's epistle to Timothy, he warns Timothy against departing from the doctrine of Christ: "If any man teach otherwise, and consent not to wholesome words, even the words of our Lord Jesus Christ, and to the doctrine which is according to godliness; He is proud, knowing nothing, but doting about questions and strifes of words, whereof cometh envy, strife, railings, evil surmisings. Perverse disputings of men of corrupt minds, and destitute of the truth, supposing that gain is godliness: from such withdraw thyself. But godliness with contentment is great gain" (1 Timothy 6:3–6).

In his epistle to the Corinthians, Paul admonished the Christian believers and cautioned them about seeking after worldly wisdom, saying, "Let no man deceive himself. If any man among you seemeth to be wise in this world, let him become a fool, that he may be wise. For the wisdom of this world is foolishness with God. For it is written, He taketh the wise in their own craftiness. And again, The Lord knoweth the thoughts of the wise, that they are vain" (1 Corinthians 3:18–20).

As valuable as philosophy is as an academic discipline, true wisdom can only come from God and His written Word. "For the Lord giveth wisdom: out of his mouth cometh knowledge and understanding" (Proverbs 2:6).

Acts 17 records Paul's trip to Athens. The spirit of God was "stirred in him" when he saw the extent to which the city was steeped in idolatry. Paul spoke God's Word daily in the synagogue, to the Judeans, and in the marketplace. Then "certain philosophers of the Epicureans and of the Stoicks" met him and asked him about this new doctrine, namely, the resurrection of Jesus Christ. In the Athenian culture, it was common practice that "all the Athenians and strangers which were there spent their time in nothing else, but either to tell, or to hear some new thing" (Acts 17:21).

Paul confronted the philosophers about their superstitious beliefs when he referred to the altar that was erected on Mars hill with the inscription "to the unknown God" (Acts 17:23).

*God that made the world and all things therein, seeing
that he is Lord of heaven and earth, dwelleth not in
temples made with hands;*
*Neither is worshipped with men's hands, as though he
needed any thing, seeing he giveth to all life, and breath,
and all things;*
*And hath made of one blood all nations of men for to
dwell on all the face of the earth, and hath determined
the times before appointed, and the bounds of their
habitation;*
*Forasmuch then as we are the offspring of God, we ought
not to think that the Godhead is like unto gold, or silver,
or stone, graven by art and man's device.*
*And the times of this ignorance God winked at; but now
commandeth all men every where to repent.*
Acts 17: 24–26, 29–30

Speaking against their idolatrous practices, Paul preached about the resurrection of Jesus Christ. Some of the philosophers mocked him, and others said, "We will hear thee again of this matter" (Acts 17:32). Paul departed from among them, and some chose to believe and "clave unto him" (Acts 17:34).

The Athenians were more concerned with their verbal and intellectual discourse in exploring "some new thing" than they were in examining the possibility that God raised Jesus Christ, His only begotten Son, from the dead. They were not interested in the "good news" but rather in argumentation and debate. But in spite of their culture, some chose to believe and became born again of God's holy spirit.

LIMITATIONS OF SENSE KNOWLEDGE

Although our five senses are important, they sometimes trick us into drawing false conclusions. Psychologists often use the Rorschach test, a series of inkblot designs, to tell us not so much about the designs themselves but rather, about the mental thoughts of the individual who interprets the designs.

Throughout the Bible, there are numerous examples of men and women who chose to walk by their senses in contrast to those who walked by the spirit of God. Although our senses are an important means of acquiring information, they are often unreliable and provide erroneous information when it comes to ascertaining spiritual truths. "But the natural man receiveth not the things of the Spirit of God: for they are foolishness unto him: neither can he know them, because they are spiritually discerned" (1 Corinthians 2:14).

What makes our five senses problematic is they are often colored by our emotions. In his insightful book, *Emotional Intelligence,* Daniel Goleman writes that we have two minds, the emotional and the rational mind. When emotions are aroused, it is the emotional mind that supersedes the rational mind; "passions overwhelm reason time and again" in what Goleman calls "emotional hijackings."[5] What is critical is not to suppress our emotions but to balance our emotional minds with our rational minds.

Human experience and culture build a repertoire of experiences, both positive and negative, in our individual lives. Often, experiences from the past continue to affect the present. It is possible, by renewing our minds to God's Word, that we can overcome the negative influences of the past and build new possibilities for the present and the future. In his epistle to the Philippians, Paul wrote, "Brethren, I count not myself to have apprehended: but this one thing I do, forgetting those things which are behind, and reaching forth unto those things which are before, I press toward the mark for the prize of the high calling of God in Christ Jesus" (Philippians 3:13–14).

Paul had a great deal that he wanted to leave behind. Prior to being born again of God's holy spirit, Paul, who was also known as Saul, persecuted the church and beat the Christian believers, hauled them off to prison, and even consented to their deaths (Acts 8:1).

Throughout the Bible, there are a number of individuals who walked by their senses. We will also look at several records where people chose to walk by the spirit of God. Fortunately, God understands the frailty and vulnerability of human beings; otherwise, He would not have given us His written Word as a guidepost to follow.

WALKING BY THE SENSES
Abraham and Isaac

Abraham is an example of a man who walked by his five senses with regard to the sacrifice of his son Isaac. Genesis 22 describes God's instructions to Abraham regarding the sacrifice of Isaac to God: "And it came to pass after these things, that God did tempt Abraham, and said unto him, Abraham: and he said, Behold, here I am. And he said, Take now thy son, thine only son Isaac, whom thou lovest, and get thee into the land of Moriah; and offer him there for a burnt offering upon one of the mountains which I will tell thee of" (Genesis 22:1–2).

The word *tempt* comes from the Hebrew word, *nasah,* and it means "to try or prove." In the Eastern custom, a burnt offering refers to a "total, unreserved commitment of self to God."[6]

God promised Abraham that he would be "the father of many nations," in Genesis 17:4–5. When Sarah was unable to bear children, she gave Abraham her Egyptian handmaid, Hagar, and willingly granted him permission to bear a child with her (Genesis 16:1–4). When Hagar bore Ishmael, Abraham assumed it was through Ishmael that God's covenant would come to pass. However, it wasn't until Abraham was approximately one hundred years old and Sarah was ninety years of age that God revealed to Abraham that His covenant would be through a son by Sarah, and the son's name would be Isaac. "I will establish my covenant with him for an everlasting covenant, and with his seed after him" (Genesis 17:19).

Some might argue that asking Abraham to offer his son as a burnt offering was a way for God to "test" Abraham's faith in Him. God, who is the searcher of all hearts (1 Chronicles 28:9) and is all-knowing, did not need to "test" Abraham regarding his faith. If God told Abraham that His "everlasting covenant" would be through Isaac, why would God have Abraham kill Isaac? James 1:13 says, "Let no man say when he is tempted, I am tempted of God: for God cannot be tempted with evil, neither tempteth he any man." Furthermore, in Romans 12:1, the Apostle Paul writes that "ye present your bodies a *living* [italics mine] sacrifice, holy, acceptable unto God, which is your reasonable service." Death is of the enemy. God's Word is carried out through men and women who are committed to walking in Christ's stead as *living* sacrifices for him. God's power cannot be manifested through a corpse.

Pagan Practices

Abraham was influenced by the culture in which he lived. He lived in the land of Canaan, where human sacrifice was a common practice among his neighbors. People in many pagan cultures slaughtered their children and sacrificed them to their gods. There were idolatrous Israelites who were also influenced by the surrounding cultures and who practiced human sacrifice that was strictly forbidden by God. The prophet Jeremiah warned God's people about these idolatrous practices:

> *And say, Hear ye the word of the Lord, O kings of Judah,*
> *and inhabitants of Jerusalem; Thus saith the Lord of hosts,*
> *the God of Israel; Behold, I will bring evil upon this place,*
> *the which whosoever heareth, his ears shall tingle.*
> *Because they have forsaken me, and have estranged this*
> *place, and have burned incense in it unto other gods,*
> *whom neither they nor their fathers have known, nor the*
> *kings of Judah, and have filled this place with the blood of*
> *innocents;*
> *They have built also the high places of Baal, to burn*
> *their sons with fire for burnt offerings unto Baal, which*
> *I commanded not, nor spake it, neither came it into my*
> *mind.*
> Jeremiah 19:3–5

Worshipping other gods and adopting the idolatrous practices of other nations was an abomination to the one true God of Israel. There are a number of records that document the Israelites' idolatrous practices and God's warnings to His people to avoid them.

> *This evil people, which refuse to hear my words, which*
> *walk in the imagination of their heart, and walk after*
> *other gods, to serve them, and to worship them, shall even*
> *be as this girdle, which is good for nothing.*

*For as the girdle cleaveth to the loins of a man, so have I
caused to cleave unto me the whole house of Israel and the
whole house of Judah, saith the Lord; that they might be
unto me for a people, and for a name, and for a praise,
and for a glory: but they would not hear.*
Jeremiah 13:10–11

*When thou art come into the land which the Lord thy
God giveth thee, thou shalt not learn to do after the
abominations of those nations.*
*There shall not be found among you any one that maketh
his son or his daughter to pass through the fire, or that
useth divination, or an observer of times, or an enchanter,
or a witch,*
*Or a charmer, or a consulter with familiar spirits, or a
wizard, or a necromancer.*
*For all that do these things are an abomination unto the
Lord: and because of these abominations the Lord thy
God doth drive them out from before thee.*
Deuteronomy 18:9–12

Over the course of time, the rulers and people of Israel
chose not to heed the God of their fathers. Rather, they chose
to walk "in the statutes of the heathen" and "did secretly those
things that were not right against the Lord their God" (2 Kings
17:8–9).

*And they left all the commandments of the Lord their
God, and made them molten images, even two calves,
and made a grove, and worshipped all the host of heaven,
and served Baal.*

And they caused their sons and their daughters to pass through the fire, and used divination and enchantments, and sold themselves to do evil in the sight of the Lord, to provoke him to anger.
2 Kings 17:16–17

They did not destroy the nations, concerning whom the Lord commanded them:
But were mingled among the heathen, and learned their works.
And they served their idols: which were a snare unto them.
Yea, they sacrificed their sons and their daughters unto devils,
And shed innocent blood, even the blood of their sons and of their daughters, whom they sacrificed unto the idols of Canaan: and the land was polluted with blood.
Thus were they defiled with their own works, and went a whoring with their own inventions.
Psalm 106:34–39

Additional references to the Israelites' idolatrous practices are recorded in Leviticus 18:21, Deuteronomy 12:30–31, Isaiah 57:5, and Jeremiah 7:31. The consequences of turning away from the one true God, practicing idolatry, and sacrificing to idols or false gods resulted in God's hand of grace and mercy being lifted from their lives. Because of their disobedience, the Israelites were brought into captivity and oppressed by their enemies (Psalm 106:40–43).[7]

Abraham was influenced by the practices of his idolatrous neighbors as well as by some of his own brethren. Erroneously thinking he was doing God's will, Abraham would have killed Isaac were it not for the intervention of an angel who prevented Isaac's death. God's will is for His children to always "choose life, that both thou and thy seed may live" (Deuteronomy 30:19). As the god of this world, the Devil's goal is always death and destruction, for "he was a murderer from the beginning" (2 Corinthians 4:4, John 8:44). Without Isaac, there would be no Jacob, and ultimately, the Christ line would have been broken.[8]

Samson and Delilah

The story of Samson is another example of a man who succumbed to his senses when he fell in love with Delilah. Judges chapters thirteen through sixteen documents the story of Samson and the Philistines' rule over Israel. There was a man of Zorah whose family was of the Danites and whose name was Manoah. Although his wife was barren, an angel appeared to her and prophesied that she would bear a son. She was further instructed that her son's hair should never be cut (Judges 13:5).

The angel advised Manoah's wife about a proper pregnancy diet. She should abstain from drinking wine or "strong drink, nor eat any unclean thing" (Judges 13:4, 14). The child was born and his parents named him Samson. Samson's life was blessed by God. As an adult, he moved to the camp of Dan and traveled to Timnath. It was at Timnath that he saw a Philistine woman and told his parents he wanted her for his wife. In spite of his parents' disapproval, Samson married the Philistine woman because "he sought an occasion against the Philistines" (Judges 14:4). In the vineyards of Timnath, he saw a young lion and killed him with his bare hands. When he returned to the vineyards, he discovered a swarm of bees and honey in the carcass of the lion. He ate the honey and shared it with his parents.

At the wedding feast, Samson posed a riddle to thirty Philistines. He challenged them and said that if they could solve a riddle, he would give them thirty sheets and thirty garments. If they could not solve the riddle, they were to give him thirty sheets and thirty garments. The riddle was, "Out of the eater came forth meat, and out of the strong came forth sweetness." The Philistines had difficulty solving the riddle and pressured Samson's bride to give them the answer. When she refused to obey them, the Philistines threatened to burn her and her father's house. After seven days of weeping and entreating Samson to give her the answer, he finally succumbed and revealed the answer to his wife who, in turn, shared it with the thirty Philistines. On the seventh day, the thirty men appeared before Samson with the question, "What is sweeter than honey and what is stronger than a lion?" Angered by their correct answer, Samson slew thirty Philistines in Ashkelon and took their garments and spoils and gave them to the other thirty Philistines in payment for correctly answering the riddle (Judges 14:18).

When he returned, he discovered that his father-in-law had given his wife to one of the thirty Philistines and offered the younger sister of Samson's wife to him. Enraged by this action, Samson caught three hundred foxes, tied torches to them, ignited the torches, and threw the foxes into the corn of the Philistines and destroyed their crops and vineyards. When the Philistines discovered that Samson had destroyed their property, they burned his wife and her father.

Clearly, Samson was a man to be reckoned with. Meanwhile, the Judeans were afraid of the Philistines because of the damage that was done to the Philistines' crops. Samson was a bold, courageous man who was not afraid of the fact that the Philistines ruled over Israel. His primary weakness was in succumbing to the seductive wiles of beautiful foreign women and giving in to their emotional persuasion.

In order to protect themselves from the retribution of the Philistines, three thousand men of Judah sought Samson, bound him with cords, and delivered him into the hands of their enemies. It was at Lehi when "the Spirit of the Lord came mightily upon him" that Samson slew a thousand men with the jawbone of an ass (Judges 15:15). Following this event, Samson judged Israel for twenty years while his people were still under the rule of the Philistines.

Samson's love for Delilah, a woman from the valley of Sorek, ultimately brought about his downfall. The Philistines were fully aware that beautiful women were Samson's weakness, and they sought the assistance of Delilah in exchange for eleven hundred pieces of silver (Judges 16:5).

On three occasions, Delilah attempted to discover the source of Samson's strength. Each time, Samson gave her a false answer. On each occasion, the Philistines discovered that Samson had deceived them. One would think that after the third time, Samson would have seen Delilah's true colors and recognized that she was collaborating with the enemy to bring about his downfall. But instead of separating himself from Delilah, he chose to remain in the relationship. As a consequence, Judges 16:16 records that "she pressed him daily with her words, and urged him, so that his soul was vexed unto death." Finally, through Delilah's sheer persistence, Samson shared his heart fully with an unbelieving woman and broke his promise to God: "That he told her all his heart, and said unto her, There hath not come a razor upon mine head; for I have been a Nazarite unto God from my mother's womb: if I be shaven, then my strength will go from me, and I shall become weak, and be like any other man" (Judges 16:17).

When Delilah heard his confession, she immediately informed the Philistines of Samson's secret. She then made Samson sleep on her knees and called a man to shave the locks of his hair. When Samson awoke, he discovered that God's spirit had departed from him. Because of his disobedience to God, the Philistines captured Samson, plucked out his eyes, and imprisoned him. Blinded and humiliated, he was made into a spectacle and was paraded before everyone during a festival in which the Philistines were planning to offer a sacrifice unto Dagon, their god. The Philistines bound Samson between two pillars of a house and continued to mock him.

During Samson's imprisonment, up to the day of the festival, the Philistines carelessly allowed Samson's hair to grow back. There were about three thousand men and women who were enjoying the festivities in the house. In a last act of courage, Samson prayed to God to strengthen him and avenge what the Philistines had done to him.

> *And Samson called unto the Lord, and said, O Lord*
> *God, remember me, I pray thee, and strengthen me, I*
> *pray thee, only this once, Oh God, that I may be at once*
> *avenged of the Philistines for my two eyes.*
> *And Samson said, Let me die with the Philistines. And*
> *he bowed himself with all his might; and the house fell*
> *upon the lords, and upon all the people that were therein.*
> *So the dead which he slew at his death were more than*
> *they which he slew in his life.*
> Judges 16:28, 30

The story of Samson describes a man of great courage and strength who "sought an occasion against the Philistines," the enemy of God's people. Unfortunately, in spite of God's grace upon his life, Samson was still a man with weaknesses. "The lust of the flesh and the lust of the eyes" (1 John 2:16) were sense knowledge responses to women who betrayed him, and ultimately brought about his downfall. In spite of walking by his senses when he succumbed to the emotional pressure of Delilah, Samson was able to prevail when he turned to God and avenged the enemies of God's people.

WALKING BY THE SPIRIT

We will now look at examples of men and women who walked by the spirit and not by the senses. In the Old Testament, there were many men and women who walked by the spirit of God. By God's grace, holy spirit could be placed upon men and women who chose to walk for God and to do His will. "I will pour out my spirit unto you, I will make known my words unto you" (Proverbs 1:23). As a searcher of the thoughts and intents of people's hearts, it was God's prerogative who would receive His spirit. If a person was disobedient and broke fellowship with God, God's spirit could be lifted from that individual's life. An example of this was when David pleaded to God not to remove the spirit of God upon him as a result of his transgression with Bathsheba. David broke fellowship with God when he impregnated Bathsheba, a married woman, and had her husband Uriah killed in battle because of his desire for Uriah's wife. David cried out to God, "Cast me not away from thy presence; and take not thy holy spirit from me" (Psalm 51:11).

Prior to the day of Pentecost, God's spirit was conditional upon men and women who chose to walk for him. Since the day of Pentecost, God's spirit is unconditional within men and women who become born again of God's holy spirit. To become born again of God's holy spirit is to receive God's incorruptible seed. Further discussion regarding this topic is described in chapter six on The Gift of Holy Spirit.

Abigail

Abigail, the wife of Nabal, was a great woman of God. Abigail was a beautiful and intelligent woman who walked by the spirit of God. In contrast, her husband was a "churlish" and evil man who belonged to the house of Caleb. "Now the name of the man was Nabal; and the name of his wife Abigail: and she was a woman of good understanding, and of a beautiful countenance: but the man was churlish and evil in his doings; and he was of the house of Caleb" (1 Samuel 25:3).

The word *churlish* comes from the Hebrew word *qasheh,* and it means "hard, harsh, and sharp." Nabal is also described as "a son of Belial" (1 Samuel 25:17).

The book of 1 Samuel 25 records that David, who was still in exile during the reign of Saul, heard that Nabal was shearing his sheep. He sent ten of his men to speak to Nabal and requested food for his men. Nabal was a wealthy man of Maon who owned sheep and goats and had more than enough to share of his plurality. David's request for food was a common occurrence in Eastern culture. For example, Abraham's generosity toward the three strangers in Genesis 18:1–8 demonstrated what was commonly expected and practiced in that culture.

Even more significant is that hospitality and kindness shown toward strangers demonstrated a person's faithfulness to God (Job 31:32, Isaiah 58:7). Failure to provide for a traveler's needs was considered to be a serious offense and a breach of etiquette.[9]

Nabal's response to David's men was a reflection of his hard heart and foolish nature: "And Nabal answered David's servants, and said, Who is David? and who is the son of Jesse? there be many servants now a days that break away every man from his master. Shall I then take my bread, and my water, and my flesh that I have killed for my shearers, and give it unto men, whom I know not whence they be?" (1 Samuel 25: 10–11).

Nabal's response was an insult of the highest degree. All of Israel knew David's reputation as a mighty man of God. As the great grandson of Ruth and Boaz and the son of Jesse, David was renowned throughout the land for having killed Goliath, the Philistine giant, with a sling and sword (1 Samuel 17:51). David was a national hero.

The men returned to David and reported what took place. Angered by this insult, David prepared to kill Nabal and his household for what was considered to be a serious breach of etiquette. One of Nabal's servants informed Abigail about what transpired. The servant also informed Abigail that while they were in the field watching over their sheep, David and his men protected them day and night.

Without informing her husband of her plan, Abigail quickly "took two hundred loaves, and two bottles of wine, five sheep ready dressed, and five measures of parched corn, and an hundred clusters of raisins, and two hundred cakes of figs, and laid them on asses" (1 Samuel 25: 18). Traveling toward David and his men, she met them on the bottom of a hill. Seeing David, she hastily bowed down and begged David to spare her household from bloodshed. Her words to David were a great example of how to win friends and influence people.

In her communication with David, Abigail acknowledged that her husband, "this man of Belial" (1 Samuel 25:25), had acted unwisely by not responding positively to David's request for food and water. She also recognized God's hand of protection and blessing upon David's life and acknowledged that he was a mighty man of God who fought the battles of the Lord (1 Samuel 25:28). Abigail begged David not to cause useless bloodshed and requested that when Nabal received the consequences of his unwise actions, David would remember her (1 Samuel 25:31).

David, being a humble man, recognized that Abigail was sent by the God of Israel to prevent him from shedding innocent blood. He then instructed her to go in peace and accepted her intercession for her household. When Abigail returned home, Nabal was in the midst of a feast and was drunk with wine. She wisely avoided telling him what happened until the next day. The following day, when Nabal was sober, Abigail informed him of the previous day's events and how close they had come to being killed, and "his heart died within him, and he became as a stone" (1 Samuel 25:37). Ten days later, Nabal died. To the wicked, the Bible says, "Therefore shall his calamity come suddenly; suddenly shall he be broken without remedy" (Proverbs 6:15). "And when David heard that Nabal was dead, he said, Blessed be the Lord, that hath pleaded the cause of my reproach from the hand of Nabal, and hath kept his servant from evil: for the Lord hath returned the wickedness of Nabal upon his own head. And David sent and communed with Abigail to take her to him to wife" (1 Samuel 25:39).

Abigail walked by the spirit of God and not by her senses. As a result of her courage, intelligence, humility, and love for God, she managed to prevent the shedding of innocent blood and ended up marrying David, a mighty man of God.

Jesus Christ
The greatest man to have walked on the face of this earth was Jesus Christ, the only begotten Son of God. "For God so loved

the world, that he gave his only begotten Son, that whosoever believeth in him should not perish, but have everlasting life. For God sent not his Son into the world to condemn the world; but that the world through him might be saved" (John 3:16–17).

When John the Baptist first beheld Jesus, he proclaimed, "Behold the Lamb of God, which taketh away the sin of the world" (John 1:29). When Jesus was baptized in the river Jordan, John witnessed the descent of the spirit and heard a voice coming from heaven saying, "Thou art my beloved Son, in whom I am well pleased" (Mark 1:9–11). "And John bare record, saying, I saw the Spirit descending from heaven like a dove, and it abode upon him. And I knew him not: but he that sent me to baptize with water, the same said unto me, Upon whom thou shalt see the Spirit descending, and remaining on him, the same is he which baptizeth with the Holy Ghost [Spirit]. And I saw, and bare record that this is the Son of God" (John 1:32–34).

God gave Jesus holy spirit without measure (John 3:34). Jesus also recognized that God's spirit was upon his life (Luke 4:18). As the Son of God, he walked with great power and authority. He challenged the religious traditions and legalisms of his day, healed the sick, and delivered people from the spiritual, mental, and physical bondage in which they were encased (Luke 4:17-21).

Even the devil spirits recognized Jesus as one who had great authority as God's spokesman. In the synagogue in Capernaum, the following record described a man with an unclean spirit: "And in the synagogue there was a man, which had a spirit of an unclean devil, and cried out with a loud voice, Saying, Let us alone; what have we to do with thee, thou Jesus of Nazareth? art thou come to destroy us? I know thee who thou are; the Holy One of God. And Jesus rebuked him, saying, Hold thy peace, and come out of him.

And when the devil had thrown him in the midst, he came out of him, and hurt him not" (Luke 4:33–35).

The people present witnessed this miracle and were amazed by the power and authority of Jesus Christ who commanded the unclean spirits to come out of the man. As Jesus healed people of many diverse diseases, "devils also came out of many, crying out, and saying, Thou art Christ the Son of God" (Luke 4:41).

Jesus gave his twelve disciples power and authority over all devil spirits to heal people of their diseases and he sent them to share the good news (Luke 9:1–2). He also appointed seventy individuals to preach the kingdom of God. When they returned with great joy, they exclaimed, "Lord, even the devils are subject unto us through thy name" (Luke 10:17). And he replied, "I beheld Satan as lightning fall from heaven. Behold, I give unto you power to tread on serpents and scorpions, and over all the power of the enemy: and nothing shall by any means hurt you" (Luke 10:18–19).

Jesus's access to spiritual knowledge came by way of God's holy spirit placed upon him and by his knowledge of the written Word. Jesus declared, "My meat is to do the will of him that sent me, and to finish his work" (John 4:34). Jesus recognized that without God, he could do nothing. The source and power of all that he had came from God. "I can of mine own self do nothing: as I hear, I judge: and my judgment is just; because I seek not mine own will, but the will of the Father which hath sent me. If I bear witness of myself, my witness is not true" (John 5:30–31).

Jesus taught that he was the bread of life and those who accepted him would never hunger or thirst. Throughout the Gospels, he continually stated, "I came down from heaven, not to do mine own will, but the will of him that sent me" (John 6:35, 38) and that "my doctrine is not mine, but his that sent me" (John 7:16).

He had a personal, intimate relationship with God, his Heavenly Father. "And he that sent me is with me: the Father hath not left me alone; for I do always those things that please him" (John 8:29). To those Judeans who believed in him, Jesus stated, "If you continue in my word, then are ye my disciples indeed; And ye shall know the truth, and the truth shall make you free" (John 8:31-32). The word *continue* is derived from the Greek word *menō,* and it means "to remain." If we remain and are faithful to God's Word, then we are disciples of Jesus Christ.

God chose Jesus as His only begotten Son in whom the gift of holy spirit was given without measure. Jesus made the decision to always do his Father's will. As a result of his life, death, resurrection, and ascension, people by their free will may choose to believe and receive remission of sins and eternal life.

> *For all have sinned, and come short of the glory of God;*
> *Being justified freely by his grace through the redemption*
> *that is in Christ Jesus:*
> *Whom God hath set forth to be a propitiation through*
> *faith in his blood, to declare his righteousness for the*
> *remission of sins that are past, through the forbearance of*
> *God.*
> Romans 3:23–25

> *Therefore being justified by faith, we have peace with*
> *God through our Lord Jesus Christ:*
> *By whom also we have access by faith into this grace*
> *wherein we stand, and rejoice in hope of the glory of God.*
> Romans 5:1–2

Jesus Christ's public ministry lasted approximately one year. He is the only person whom God raised from the dead and who is now sitting on the right hand of God (Colossians 3:1, Hebrews 10:12, Hebrews 12:2, 1 Peter 3:22). This same power that raised Jesus Christ from the dead is now available in our day and time to those who believe Romans 10:9-10. Jesus proclaimed this truth in the book of John: "Verily, verily, I say unto you, He that believeth on me, the works that I do shall he do also; and greater works than these shall he do; because I go unto my Father" (John 14:12).

The gift of holy spirit became available on the day of Pentecost and is freely available today to those who hunger and thirst after righteousness (Matthew 5:6, Acts 1:8, 2:4).

> *Come unto me, all ye that labour and are heavy laden,*
> *and I will give you rest.*
> *Take my yoke upon you, and learn of me; for I am meek*
> *and lowly in heart: and ye shall find rest unto your souls.*
> *For my yoke is easy, and my burden is light.*
> Mathew 11:28–30

> *These things I have spoken unto you, that in me ye*
> *might have peace.*
> *In the world ye shall have tribulation: but be of good*
> *cheer; I have overcome the world.*
> John 16:33

In this chapter, we looked at sense knowledge versus spiritual knowledge. As valuable as our five senses are, they are limited in scope and possibilities. Dealing with personal challenges, such as finding a job, acquiring financial security, overcoming a disease, or even finding a helpmate involves acquiring a spiritual perspective in knowing that God is our sufficiency. Walking with spiritual knowledge is choosing to believe and act upon God's Word. Regardless of circumstances, as we believe, God will absolutely bring to pass the desires of our hearts according to His written Word.

We saw examples from the Bible of choices that Abraham and Samson made when they chose to walk by their five senses. We also saw the results of Abigail and Jesus Christ when they chose to walk by the spirit of God. As we renew our minds to God's Word, and learn how to operate the gift of holy spirit, we too, can see great deliverance in our lives when we choose to believe and act upon the Word of God. In the next chapter, we will witness the power that became available on the day of Pentecost, which was freely given to those who chose to be born again of God's holy spirit.

PRACTICAL KEYS TO APPLYING THE BIBLE

1. Document those victories in your life when you chose to believe the promises in the Bible as opposed to the negative circumstances in the world.

2. Write down your personal and spiritual goals and use a Bible concordance to document the scriptures that will build your believing images of victory for God's deliverance in your life.

3. Eliminate your associations with negative people who tear down your positive believing and discourage you from claiming the promises in the Bible.

4. Associate with positive, encouraging people who believe in, speak of, and who are living examples of the Word of God in operation.

5. Identify and eliminate fears from your life by replacing those fears with positive scriptures from the Bible.

6. Continue to tithe and abundantly share your finances that God has blessed you with.

SCRIPTURES FOR FURTHER STUDY

Genesis 18:14
Proverbs 27:17

2 Corinthians 6:14
Ephesians 1:19
Ephesians 3:20
Philippians 1:6
Philippians 2:13
Philippians 4:6–8

CHAPTER SIX

THE GIFT OF HOLY SPIRIT

But ye shall receive power, after that the Holy Ghost [Spirit] is come
upon you: and ye shall be witnesses unto me both in Jerusalem, and
in all Judea, and in Samaria, and unto the uttermost part of the earth.
Acts 1:8

THE COMPETITIVE EDGE

Athletes want it. Politicians crave it. Financial managers wish they had it. What is it that most people yearn for in life? It's the competitive edge. In the competitive world of job seeking, moneymaking, relationship building, sports competition, power building, or just plain winning in life, people are always looking for that edge that places them ahead of the pack.

What about in the spiritual arena of life? What if your opponent is invisible and powerful, has a thorough knowledge of your weaknesses, breeds on your fears and insecurities, is capable of manipulating people, culture, and the environment, and is intent on stealing, killing, and destroying? How would you overcome such a formidable adversary? In the spiritual competition, pedigree doesn't matter, degrees don't count, money has no impact, nor does cultural background. The only thing that will back down your spiritual opponent is the spiritual power from God that comes from being born again of God's holy spirit. Fleshly tools have little power or impact over the spiritual realm.

ATHLETES OF THE SPIRIT

In the Old Testament, the Israelites, after they crossed the Jordan River, engaged in a military competition and fought against their enemies. Their opponents were the Canaanites, Hittites, Hivites, Perizzites, Girgashites, Amorites, and Jebusites (Joshua 3:10). They also fought against the Amalekites and the Ammonites, and even Samson sought an occasion to do battle with the Philistines.

As described in the New Testament epistles, from Romans to Thessalonians, our conflict is not against a physical opponent but against a spiritual adversary. "For though we walk in the flesh, we do not war after the flesh: For the weapons of our warfare are not carnal, but mighty through God to the pulling down of strong holds" (2 Corinthians 10:3-4). The following scriptures use athletic terminology to describe the spiritual competition we face.

> *Know ye not that they which run in a race run all, but one receiveth the prize? So run, that ye may obtain. And every man that striveth for the mastery is temperate in all things. Now they do it to obtain a corruptible crown; but we an incorruptible.*
> 1 Corinthians 9:24–25

> *I therefore so run, not as uncertainly; so fight I, not as one that beateth the air: But I keep my body, and bring it into subjection: lest that by any means, when I have preached to others, I myself should be a castaway.*
> 1 Corinthians 9:26–27

For we wrestle not against flesh and blood, but against principalities, against powers, against the rulers of the darkness of this world, against spiritual wickedness in high places.
Ephesians 6:12

Hebrews also documents the physical competition of the race that is set before us: "Wherefore seeing we also are compassed about with so great a cloud of witnesses, let us lay aside every weight, and the sin which doth so easily beset us, and let us run with patience the race that is set before us" (Hebrews 12:1).

Our opponent is a spiritual adversary who steals, kills, and destroys. It is impossible to kill spirit. Ultimately, the lake of fire awaits the Devil and his cohort of devil spirits (Mathew 25:41, Revelation 19:20). "For this purpose the Son of God was manifested, that he might destroy the works of the devil" (1 John 3:8b). The word *destroy* comes from the Greek word *luo,* and it means "to loosen or break up by component parts." Until Jesus Christ returns, what we are called to do is dismantle or break up by component parts the Devil's works, as Jesus Christ did when he was alive on earth.

As we faithfully apply and live the principles of God's Word, share God's Word with others, and run "the race that is set before us," we will be rewarded with incorruptible crowns for living a life that glorifies God and our Lord Jesus Christ.

Oppressed by the Romans, the Israelites wanted a political or military leader to lead them out of bondage. Jesus Christ was neither a military nor a political leader. He is the Son of God who came to restore the lost sheep of the house of Israel back to God (Mathew 10:6, Mathew 15:24, Romans 15:8). As a result of his life, crucifixion, death, resurrection, and ascension, those who confess Jesus as Lord and believe that God raised him from the dead are born again of God's holy spirit and receive all enablements to stand against our spiritual adversary, the Devil (Romans 10:9–10).

WHAT IS HOLY SPIRIT?

God, who is Spirit, can only give of Himself which is the gift of holy spirit; "and they that worship him must worship him in spirit and in truth" (John 4:24).

Jesus taught his disciples in John 14:16 that they would receive a Comforter that would abide with them forever. During his ministry, Jesus Christ received the spirit of God without measure (John 3:34). The foretelling of a Comforter, or Holy Spirit, is expressed in the following passages:

> *And I will pray the Father, and he shall give you another*
> *Comforter, that he may abide with you for ever;*
> *Even the Spirit of truth; whom the world cannot receive,*
> *because it seeth him not, neither knoweth him: but ye*
> *know him; for he dwelleth with you, and shall be in you.*
> John 14:16–17

> *But the Comforter, which is the Holy Ghost [Spirit],*
> *whom the Father will send in my name, he shall teach*
> *you all things, and bring all things to your remembrance,*
> *whatsoever I have said unto you.*
> John 14:26

Jesus taught that in order for the Comforter to come, it was necessary that he go away: "for if I go not away, the Comforter will not come unto you; but if I depart, I will send him unto you" (John 16:7b).

The book of Acts describes the instructions that Jesus Christ gave to the twelve disciples before his ascension. He instructed them on the day of the ascension that they were not to leave Jerusalem "but wait for the promise of the Father" (Acts 1:4). John baptized with water, but they would be baptized with the gift of holy spirit (Acts 1:5).

The second chapter of the book of Acts describes a supernatural event that took place on the day of Pentecost. As the disciples were sitting "with one accord in one place…there came a sound from heaven as of a rushing mighty wind," and they were filled with the holy spirit and began to speak with other tongues "as the Spirit gave them utterance" (Acts 2:1–2, 4). People from other nations were present when this miraculous event took place. They were confounded and amazed because the disciples were from Galilee, and yet they spoke in other languages. "And they were all amazed and marveled, saying one to another, Behold, are not all these which speak Galileans? And how hear we every man in our own tongue, wherein we were born? Parthians, and Medes, and Elamites, and the dwellers in Mesopotamia, and in Judea, and Cappadocia, in Pontus, and Asia, Phrygia, and Pamphylia, in Egypt, and in the parts of Libya about Cyrene, and strangers of Rome, Jews and proselytes, Cretes and Arabians, we do hear them speak in our tongues the wonderful works of God" (Acts 2:7–11).

The people present proclaimed that the disciples were speaking "the wonderful works of God." There were a few who mocked the disciples and accused them of being drunk with wine (Acts 2:13). In the midst of these accusations, Peter boldly stood up and confronted the accusers. He stated that Jesus of Nazareth, whom they crucified, God raised from the dead and made both Lord and Christ (Acts 2:21–36). On that day, approximately three thousand people were baptized in the name of Jesus Christ, received remission of sins, and were born again of God's holy spirit (Acts 2:38–41).

RECEIVING THE GIFT OF HOLY SPIRIT

What does it mean to be born again and receive the gift of holy spirit? How difficult of a process is it? Can anyone be born again and receive the gift of holy spirit?

As a result of faithfully attending a Bible fellowship since 1984, and enrolling in Bible classes, I learned that being born again of God's holy spirit is a simple process. It isn't necessary to run down the aisle and confess my sins to an intermediary or perform a series of good works. God's love for us is unconditional and comes by grace and mercy. "For by grace are ye saved through faith; and that not of yourselves: it is the gift of God: Not of works, lest any man should boast. For we are his workmanship, [masterpiece] created in Christ Jesus unto good works, which God hath before ordained that we should walk in them" (Ephesians 2:8–10).

Being born again of God's holy spirit is to confess Jesus Christ as Lord in your life and believe that God raised him from the dead. "That if thou shalt confess with thy mouth the Lord Jesus, and shalt believe in thine heart that God hath raised him from the dead, thou shalt be saved. For with the heart man believeth unto righteousness; and with the mouth confession is made unto salvation" (Romans 10:9–10).

Acting on Romans 10:9–10 gives us free access to the grace, mercy, power, and riches of our heavenly Father. I am thankful to have learned this simple truth. If I were rewarded for my works, it would take me forever to receive God's gift of holy spirit. My imperfections and mistakes would continue to weigh me down. Thank God there is a simpler way to break the endless cycle of self-condemnation and errors made in life.

Jesus Christ gave his life so we could receive remission of sins and physical wholeness. He removed all obstacles that separated us from God. God, through His only begotten Son, gave us the ultimate gift of eternal life. When you become born again of God's holy spirit, you have Christ within, the hope of glory. "To whom God would make known what is the riches of the glory of this mystery among the Gentiles; which is Christ in you, the hope of glory" (Colossians 1:27).

God's will is for everyone to be saved "and to come unto the knowledge of the truth" (1 Timothy 2:4). In spite of this gift, there are those who still try to earn their own salvation. In fact, some religions believe that through the process of rebirth, a person lives successive lives and works out his or her salvation through good works and self-purification.[1]

However, God knew it was impossible to live perfectly, and even more difficult to earn our own salvation, because "all have sinned, and come short of the glory of God" (Romans 3:23). "Therefore by the deeds of the law there shall no flesh be justified in his sight: for by the law is the knowledge of sin. But now the righteousness of God without the law is manifested, being witnessed by the law and the prophets; Even the righteousness of God which is by faith of Jesus Christ unto all and upon all them that believe; for there is no difference: For all have sinned, and come short of the glory of God" (Romans 3:20–23).

The Bible declares that "Christ is the end of the law for righteousness to every one that believeth" (Romans 10:4).

Believing is the key to appropriating the blessings of God. Jesus Christ is the mediator between humanity and God (1 Timothy 2:5). Some might question why God selected Jesus Christ to be His only begotten Son. Why did God select Abel's offering rather than Cain's? Why did God choose David, the youngest son of Jesse, rather than Eliab, to succeed Saul to reign over Israel? God gave this explanation to the prophet Samuel when He refused Eliab: "Look not on his countenance, or on the height of his stature; because I have refused him: for the Lord seeth not as man seeth; for man looketh on the outward appearance, but the Lord looketh on the heart" (1 Samuel 16:7).

Why did God have Jesus Christ born of the lineage of Abraham, Isaac, and Jacob and not from another tribe of Israel? Paul, by revelation, wrote in Romans 9:7, "In Isaac shall thy seed be called." "For he saith to Moses, I will have mercy on whom I will have mercy, and I will have compassion on whom I will have compassion. So then it is not of him that willeth, nor of him that runneth, but of God that sheweth mercy" (Romans 9:15–16).

God reinforces this truth in Isaiah 55:8-9: "For my thoughts are not your thoughts, neither are your ways my ways, saith the Lord. For as the heavens are higher than the earth, so are my ways higher than the earth, so are my ways higher than your ways, and my thoughts than your thoughts."

People can argue about and question God's decisions till the end of time. Regardless of human beings' opinions, argumentation and debate will not change the outcome of what is, what shall be, or what has already transpired.

If receiving the gift of holy spirit is such a simple process, why haven't more people received this gift from God? Paul's epistle written to the Corinthian church highlights some of the challenges that believers face today. Corinthians was written to correct the practical error that crept into the church because the believers failed to adhere to the revelation in the book of Romans. In the following passage, Paul writes about the simplicity of believing in Jesus Christ and the distinction between worldly wisdom and the wisdom of God:

> For Christ sent me not to baptize, but to preach the gospel: not with wisdom of words, lest the cross of Christ should be made of none effect.
> For the preaching of the cross is to them that perish foolishness; but unto us which are saved it is the power of God.
> For it is written, I will destroy the wisdom of the wise, and will bring to nothing the understanding of the prudent.
> Where is the wise? where is the scribe? where is the disputer of this world? hath not God made foolish the wisdom of this world?
> For after that in the wisdom of God the world by wisdom knew not God, it pleased God by the foolishness of preaching to save them that believe.
> For the Jews [Judeans] require a sign, and the Greeks seek after wisdom:
> But we preach Christ crucified, unto the Jews [Judeans] a stumblingblock, and unto the Greeks foolishness.
> 1 Corinthians 1:17–23

BARRIERS TO RECEIVING HOLY SPIRIT
Wrong Teaching and Ignorance

Victor Paul Wierwille, in *Receiving the Holy Spirit Today*,[2] writes that most fears that prevent the receiving of the gift of holy spirit into manifestation are either due to wrong teaching or ignorance of the Word of God. There are some who believe that the phenomenon of receiving the holy spirit died with the apostles or that it is for a select few. There are also those who feel unworthy because of the erroneous belief that they are not good enough to receive this gift from God.

Today, there are thousands of Christian denominations with varying beliefs about the gift of holy spirit. Each has its own view regarding who can and cannot receive this free gift from God. There are those who maintain that speaking in tongues "died with the apostles" or worse yet, comes from the Devil. Many Christians may be born again but were never taught about the nine manifestations of holy spirit or that they are capable, by their own free will, of operating the manifestations.

When I was a little girl attending Sunday school, I don't remember learning that I could be born again and receive the gift of holy spirit simply by believing Romans 10:9–10. I didn't know this gift was available, nor did I understand the spiritual significance and the inherent power resulting from being born again. It wasn't until I enrolled in Bible classes that I learned how to receive the gift of holy spirit and learned what was freely available to me as a born-again believer. Sadly, many people go through life without experiencing the living reality and power of manifesting this perfect gift from God.

Peter taught in Acts 10:34 that "God is no respecter of persons." Anyone who has the desire to know God, and who accepts Jesus Christ as Lord, can be born again of God's holy spirit and experientially operate the power of God.

Pride

Proverbs 16:18 warns, "Pride goeth before destruction, and an haughty spirit before a fall." Just as Lucifer, the Devil, fell because of pride, there are those who choose to elevate themselves above God in their attempt to earn their own salvation and eternal life. Protagoras, a well-known teacher in ancient Greece, reflects this egocentric philosophy when he states, "man is the measure of all things: of things that are, that they are; and of things that are not, that they are not." In contrast, Proverbs 16:19 declares, "Better it is to be of an humble spirit with the lowly, than to divide the spoil with the proud." First Peter 5:5 says, "God resisteth the proud, and giveth grace to the humble."

Today, we see the results of people who elevate themselves above others. Our society is filled with examples of pride, greed, and an egocentric mentality of being above the law. Corruption on Wall Street, in insurance, banking, and the automobile industry are warning signs symptomatic of a society that something has gone terribly wrong. Outrageous executive bonuses given out at the expense of, and on the backs of honest, hardworking Americans compel us to ask by what standards are the leaders of our political, economic, and financial institutions operating from? Clearly, they are not the standards of God's written Word.

Fear

"The fear of man bringeth a snare: but whoso putteth his trust in the Lord shall be safe" (Proverbs 29:25). A snare is a device that consists of a noose for capturing birds or small animals. It is a trap that is invisible to the naked eye, and is designed to entangle or catch its prey unawares. God is trying to make a point here.

Due to wrong teaching or ignorance, people can be fearful of what they haven't been exposed to. How does a person distinguish between a genuine manifestation of holy spirit and a counterfeit spiritual experience? Because the Devil is also a spirit, a person can be possessed with a devil spirit, or multiple spirits, for that matter, as described in different records in the Bible.[3]

I recall reading a newspaper account of a young man who said he heard voices in his head ordering him to kill his father. Tragically, the teenager obeyed the voices and thrust a sword into his sleeping father's chest. 1 John 4:1 warns us not to believe every spirit: "Beloved, believe not every spirit, but try the spirits whether they are of God; because many false prophets are gone out into the world." The standard of the written Word must be the litmus test between the genuine manifestations of holy spirit and a counterfeit spiritual experience. Isaiah 8:20 reminds us of this truth: "If they speak not according to this word, it is because *there is no light in them*" [italics mine]. Rationality, logic, and the truth of God's Word should govern our actions; not fantasy, daydreaming, or delusions of power.

We can distinguish between a genuine and a counterfeit spiritual experience by the fruit it produces. Galatians 5:22–23 says, the "fruit of the Spirit is love, joy, peace, long-suffering, gentleness, goodness, faith, meekness, temperance: against such there is no law." The genuine fruit of holy spirit expressed in Galatians 5:22–23 must be contrasted against the fruit of one's actions.

"For God is not the author of confusion, but of peace, as in all churches of the saints" (1 Corinthians 14:33). James 3:16 says, "where envying and strife is, there is confusion, and every evil work." The Bible states, "Let all things be done decently and in order" (1 Corinthians 14:40). God is the author of peace and order, never of confusion and chaos.

All that God is, the Devil is the antithesis of. Desiring to be worshipped like the one true God, the Devil counterfeits the manifestations of holy spirit by seducing and beguiling people with false signs and lying wonders. Having an accurate knowledge of God's Word eliminates fear from our lives.

MANIFESTATIONS OF HOLY SPIRIT

There are nine manifestations of holy spirit that are available to every born-again believer (1 Corinthians 12:7–10). The nine manifestations of holy spirit are divided into three categories:[4]

1. **Utterance, Speaking, Worship, Inspirational Manifestations**
    B. Speaking in tongues
    C. Interpretation of tongues
    D. Prophecy
2. **Revelation, Information, Instructional, Knowing Manifestations**
    C. Word of knowledge
    D. Word of wisdom
    E. Discerning of spirits
3. **Action, Power, Impartation Manifestations**
    D. Faith (believing)
    E. Workings of miracles
    F. Gifts of healings

The gift of holy spirit and the nine manifestations are profitable to every individual (1 Corinthians 12:7). Believing is the key to manifesting this gift. Wierwille writes:

> *God energizes all manifestations in every believer, but the believer may manifest, in the Church, one of the manifestations more effectively according to his own believing, for the benefit of all.*

*God gives the gift which is spirit; but once given, it is
the recipient of the gift, the spirit-filled believer, who is
responsible for its operation.*

*The evidences of the gift, the holy spirit, pneuma hagion,
in the spirit-filled believer in the senses world are according
to each man's believing. God is more anxious to give
than we are to receive. At this point, our believing, not
God, makes possible the reality of our receiving into
manifestation.*[5]

Utterance, Speaking, Worship, Inspirational Manifestations

The purpose of the inspirational manifestations of speaking
in tongues, interpretation of tongues, and prophecy is to edify,
exhort, and comfort the body of believers. When properly manifested, the person who is fully instructed may be called upon at a
fellowship meeting to speak in tongues and provide an interpretation in a language that the people present can understand. The
message that is brought forth will edify those who are present at
the fellowship meeting.

I was intrigued when I first heard about the manifestation of
speaking in tongues. Speaking in tongues does not involve a language that you learn, like French, German, or Spanish. Imagine
acquiring a foreign language without ever having to study for it!
The Bible says that speaking in tongues is of men or of angels
(1 Corinthians 13:1). Speaking in tongues is the evidence in the
senses realm that you are born again of God's holy spirit and that
you have eternal life.

When I attended my first Bible fellowship, I observed that
the manifestations of speaking in tongues, the interpretation of
tongues, and the bringing forth of a word of prophecy were carried out in a peaceful and orderly manner. The manifestations of

holy spirit were edifying and encouraging to everyone present. As I continued my biblical studies, I, too, learned how to operate the worship manifestations. When I spoke in tongues in my private prayer life, I found that it brought rest to my soul. Speaking in tongues helped me to stay peaceful, so I could focus on the positive promises from God's Word.

What Speaking in Tongues is Not

Speaking in tongues is a *free will* choice that the individual makes to manifest the power of God. The operation of this manifestation of holy spirit is not possession, it is not being "slain in the spirit," nor is it speaking gibberish with no godly results. Speaking in tongues is not linguistic ability but rather, "it is an inspired expression of a language which may or may not be understood by people somewhere in the world (1 Corinthians 13:1)."[6]

Speaking in tongues does not require a knowledge of known languages nor an understanding of foreign languages. And finally, speaking in tongues is not yelling, speaking incoherently, or making strange noises. Wierwille writes that "speaking in tongues is the God-given spiritual ability to speak in other tongues at will as the Spirit gives utterance." Each believer determines, by his or her free will decision, to speak in tongues.

Benefits of Speaking in Tongues

When speaking in tongues is manifested and interpreted, those present are edified and reminded of the promises in God's Word. The person who is called upon to speak in tongues also provides an interpretation of what is spoken in a language that everyone present can understand. The interpretation never contradicts the Word of God. Some of the benefits derived from speaking in tongues are as follows:[7]

- To be edified—1 Corinthians 14:4; Jude 20
- To speak divine secrets to God—1 Corinthians 14:2
- To speak the wonderful works of God—Acts 2:11
- To magnify God—Acts 10:46
- To pray perfectly—Romans 8:26–27
- To give thanks well—1 Corinthians 14:17
- To have the Spirit bearing witness with your spirit—Romans 8:16
- To know you are a joint-heir with Christ—Romans 8:17
- To strengthen you with might in your inner man—Ephesians 3:16, 2 Corinthians 4:16
- To be a sign to unbelievers—1 Corinthians 14:22, Mark 16:17
- To bring rest to the soul—Isaiah 28:11–12, 1 Corinthians 14:21
- To bring a message from God to the people when interpreted—1 Corinthians 14:4-5, 13, 27, 28

The Apostle Paul recognized the importance of speaking in tongues when he wrote, "I thank my God, I speak with tongues more than ye all" (1 Corinthians 14:18). The revelation that God gave Paul when he wrote the church epistles is a testimony of the power that comes from operating this manifestation of holy spirit. In a Bible fellowship, a word of prophecy may also be spoken by another believer to edify and comfort the Body of Christ. When there are genuine manifestations of speaking in tongues, interpretation of tongues, and bringing forth a word of prophecy, the believers present are encouraged and strengthened with the Word of God.

Revelation, Information, Instructional, and Knowing Manifestations

An example of the operation of the manifestation of word of knowledge occurred when Peter confronted Ananias about holding back part of the price of the land that Ananias and his wife, Sapphira, sold. Peter's confrontation in Acts 5:1–10 revealed Ananias' deception. When confronted with the truth, Ananias dropped dead out of fear. About three hours later, Sapphira appeared, and Peter confronted her with their deception, and she "fell down straightway at his feet, and yielded up the ghost." By way of the manifestation of word of knowledge, God was able to provide Peter with information that he would not have known by his five senses.

When Paul and Silas were at Philippi, "a certain damsel possessed with a spirit of divination" followed them for several days and cried, "These men are the servants of the most high God, which shew unto us the way of salvation" (Acts 16:16–18). By operating word of knowledge, word of wisdom, and discerning of spirits, Paul commanded, in the name of Jesus Christ, that the spirit come out of the woman, and it came out of her that very same hour.

Revelational, informational, instructional, and knowing manifestations, given by God, can be operated by any born-again believer to deal with life's challenges. These manifestations are not for the purpose of winning the lottery, nor are they designed to fulfill a person's egotistical desire for power, fame, or glory. There are a number of instances in my own life where God was able to protect me from harm. Sometimes it is a "still, small voice" instructing me to go in another direction. On other occasions,

I may experience an uneasy feeling when I meet certain people. In those instances, God is warning me that I should stay away from certain individuals. I may also experience a spiritual heaviness when there are oppressive or depressing spirits that are present in a person's life or in a geographical location. Because we are individuals, God communicates with us in a personal manner that we can understand.

The holy spirit that is given to you when you are born again is unique to you as an individual. "For it is God which worketh in you both to will and to do of his good pleasure" (Philippians 2:13). Walking by the spirit of God and learning to operate the gift of holy spirit takes humility, faithfulness, patience, and experience. The more of the Word of God that you learn, the greater the extent to which God is able to work within you. *Remember, properly operating the manifestations of holy spirit will never contradict the Word of God.*

It is God's prerogative to give a believer word of knowledge, word of wisdom, and discerning of spirits. The purpose for giving this information is to benefit and protect the individual, to strengthen the body of believers, to bring deliverance to the lives of others, and to glorify God.

Has there ever been a time when God directed you not to go down a particular path or kept you out of harm's way? The following incident is a true story communicated to the author by a believer logging in the Colorado mountains. This example exemplifies the power of prayer, believing, and being humble to God's guidance.

> *I was logging high in the Rocky Mountains to get the standing-dead spruce that was needed for a building in Gunnison, Colorado. With me was a crew of believers dedicated to getting the job done. We had only a matter of weeks to complete the logging, and so every*

day's work had to count. When we were partway through the job, it began raining. And it rained every day for about two weeks. Obviously, these were not the best conditions for getting logs out of the forest in a timely way. So we prayed together specifically for a few things: to complete the task and to work in comfort and in safety. Well, it kept raining. What did change was our attitude about the rain. We decided that the weather would not stop our progress. Our determination increased, as did our attitude. We became even stronger in our believing that we would get the whole job done and done on time. "Comfort" soon became a state of mind.

One day, while in this logging process, I was attaching a large metal cable (called a choker) to some trees that had been cut and were lying on the ground. The felled trees were one hundred plus feet long and larger at the base than a man could stretch his arms around. I would attach the trees with the strong cables to the back of a machine called a "skidder," a tall, noisy piece of equipment with thick tires taller than most people, and pull them across the steep hillside and undergrowth. The skidder was jointed in the middle to allow the front end to turn independently from the rear end so that it could make sharp turns around obstacles in the woods.

Not too far from my work area, there was another member of the crew doing the same thing. As the other man was dragging his logs through the woods, his load pushed up against some standing trees still rooted in the hillside. By now, after days of rain, the ground was so saturated with water that the roots were weak and couldn't hold the trees upright. No one realized that the impact of the trees being dragged along behind the large piece of equipment would actually dislodge any of the standing trees. As I stooped over to put the choker around the base of a cut tree, there was an abrupt shout nearby that caught my attention. The sound of a loud, abrasive "HEY!" made me stand up straight and look around. Just then, an immense spruce with full branches came crashing down immediately in front of me, so close that it brushed off my hat. Had I still been bent over choking the logs, I would have been pinned to the ground by the force of the falling tree. I stood there, stunned, and curious as to who had yelled to save my life. No one was watching; no one was speaking. The forest was silent except for the other log skidder now far in the distance, snaking its load out to the road.

Later, during lunch, while the men gathered around a campfire to dry their clothes, I asked if anyone had called my name at any time during the morning. No one had, which is what I had concluded when I found myself alone, facing the massive tree that landed at my feet. Only God could have arrested my attention that quickly and that precisely to save me from harm.

This incident illustrates that God's guidance and protection are always available to us when we trust and obey. Death is an enemy, never a friend. As we walk by the spirit of God, He can and will protect us and keep us out of harm's way.

Action, Power, and Impartation Manifestations

In order to operate the action, power, and impartation manifestations, faith (believing) must occur before a miracle and/or healing takes place. In Acts 3, Peter and John went up to the temple to pray (Acts 3:1). A man who was crippled from his mother's womb lay at the temple gate called "Beautiful," to ask alms of the people who entered there. When Peter and John passed by, the lame man reached out to them to ask for alms. The man had to first take the believing action to reach out to Peter and John. Peter instructed the man to "look on us."

In other words, Peter wanted the man to focus his attention on him. The lame man did so, "expecting to receive something of them."

Then Peter said, Silver and gold have I none; but such as I have give I thee: In the name of Jesus Christ of Nazareth rise up and walk.

And he took him by the right hand, and lifted him up: and immediately his feet and ancle bones received strength.

And he leaping up stood, and walked, and entered with them into the temple, walking, and leaping, and praising God.

And all the people saw him walking and praising God.
Acts 3:6–9

It is important to note that the utterance, revelation, and action manifestations of holy spirit are not separate entities. In turning his attention to the lame man, Peter operated the manifestations of word of knowledge and word of wisdom. Peter then received revelation from God to instruct the lame man to "look on us." When the lame man did so, the spirit of God was energized in Peter to speak the words, "In the name of Jesus Christ of Nazareth rise up and walk." Great believing had to take place on the part of the lame man to follow the instructions that Peter gave him, as he physically took the believing action to rise up, and then the miracle of healing took place. Miracles and healings were common occurrences in the book of Acts, "and by the hands of the apostles were many signs and wonders wrought among the people" (Acts 5:12).

During the gospel period, Jesus performed many miracles and healings. In one particular record, a father brought his son who was possessed to Jesus, requesting that his son be healed. Prior to this, the father had sought the help of Jesus's disciples, but they had been unable to cast the spirit out of the young boy. When the father asked Jesus for his help, Jesus's response was, "If thou canst believe, all things are possible to him that believeth" (Mark 9:23). Why were the disciples unable to heal the man's son? Jesus spiritually discerned that the obstacle to the boy's healing was not with the disciples but lay with the father's lack of believing. With the exception of certain types of mental derangement in the person to be healed, where the person is a child, or the person is dead, believing is required on the part of the recipient in order for the miracle of healing to take place.[8] In this instance, the father needed to believe for the deliverance of his young son. In recognizing this truth, the father's response was, "Lord, I believe; help thou mine unbelief" (Mark 9:24). Jesus was then able to cast out the spirit and heal the young child.

The power of believing and its influence on healing are being addressed in contemporary medicine. Doctors recognize the power of prayer and faith and its impact on recovery and healing. Dr. Mehmet Oz, a surgeon, writes that "the answers to wellness often lie within the patient." He found that an anesthetized patient undergoing open heart surgery could hear sounds during surgery. Other studies conducted demonstrated that guided imagery audiotapes can alter bleeding rates and the mind can even control the stickiness of blood.[9]

Healings and miracles are as readily available today as they were in the first-century Church. Great deliverance is available as we apply the Word of God because signs follow those who believe (Mark 16:17). It is important to remember that medical care should be sought when it is needed. But prayer can, and should work hand in hand with proper medical attention.

FREE WILL DECISION

Being born again of God's holy spirit is a free will decision. God never possesses or controls an individual. By our free will choice, we can receive into manifestation the gift of holy spirit. What we choose to do with this gift, like everything else, is also a free will decision. Victor Paul Wierwille writes:

> *The gift of holy spirit is never given on the basis of human merit, but on the basis of grace, as the Bible so clearly teaches. Immediately after receiving the holy spirit, power from on high, a man has no more Christian character than he had the moment before he received, but he now has the source of help and the ability to bring forth spiritual fruit, and this cannot be overvalued.*
> *Men are known by their fruit, and not by the gifts they possess. Gifts are no proof of good character. Gifts are received in a moment of time by believing, but producing fruit is growth in disciplined Christian living.* [10]

POWER TO DESTROY THE WORKS OF THE DEVIL

The gift of holy spirit is freely given to every born-again believer to utilize, because God knew we needed this power to deal with a formidable adversary. Jesus appointed seventy disciples to go out and speak God's Word to others. "The harvest truly is great, but the labourers are few: pray ye therefore the Lord of the harvest, that he would send forth labourers into his harvest" (Luke 10:1–2).

Following their return, the disciples had great joy in their hearts, because they discovered that even the devil spirits were subject unto them through the name of Jesus (Luke 10:17).

Prior to the day of Pentecost, the seventy disciples were given spiritual power to destroy the works of the Devil. Although they were not born again of God's holy spirit, because the day of Pentecost had not yet arrived, they were able to utilize the power that Jesus gave them to "tread on serpents and scorpions, and over all the power of the enemy" (Luke 10:19). The "serpents and scorpions" are figures of speech representing the devil spirit realm and its devilish influences. Jesus, who had God's Spirit without measure, was able to give this spiritual power to his seventy disciples (John 3:34–35). They had spirit *upon* them.

The same power made available on the day of Pentecost is now available to every born-again believer. As born-again believers, we have received God's incorruptible seed, God's holy spirit *within* us. The gift of holy spirit is freely given to us to destroy the works of the Devil. We are to do the works of Jesus Christ and greater works, as described in John 14:12.[11] We have the responsibility to reconcile men and women back to God and to dismantle, by component parts, the works of the Devil. "He that committeth sin is of the devil; for the devil sinneth from the beginning. For this purpose the Son of God was manifested, that he might destroy the works of the devil" (1 John 3:8).

PRACTICAL KEYS TO APPLYING THE BIBLE

1. Document those instances in your life when you listened to that "still, small voice" and God protected you from harm.

2. Record those instances when you ignored that "still, small voice" and got into trouble as a result of responding with your sense knowledge.

3. Faithfully tithe and abundantly share your finances with the organization that teaches you God's Word. With an attitude of gratitude, document the blessings that God brings to pass in your life.

4. Faithfully read the Bible and enroll in Bible classes to grow in spiritual knowledge and strength.

5. Walking by the spirit requires humility, faithfulness, time, and patience. Avoid seeking after "signs and wonders." In a journal, describe the blessings you receive as you faithfully apply the principles you are learning from the Bible.

SCRIPTURES FOR FURTHER STUDY

John 16:13
Acts 1:8
Acts 2:17

Acts 4:33

1 Timothy 4:1–5

1 John 4:1–4

CHAPTER SEVEN

RENEWED MIND
THE KEY TO POWER

And be not conformed to this world: but be ye
transformed by the renewing of your mind, that
ye may prove what is that good, and acceptable,
and perfect will of God.
Romans 12:2

One who brings a mind not to be chang'd by Place
or Time. The mind is its own place, and in it self
Can make a Heav'n of Hell, a Hell of Heav'n.
What matter where, if I be still the same....
Lucifer, in *Paradise Lost*
John Milton

Renewing your mind in the midst of pain and suffering is not an easy task. When confronted with an emotionally charged situation, and your mind is ready to explode, it is wiser to use restraint rather than succumb to your volatile emotions.

The spiritual competition is in the mind. Henry Thoreau wrote, "we should treat our minds, that is, ourselves, as innocent and ingenuous children, whose guardians we are, and be careful what objects and what subjects we thrust on their attention. Read not the Times. Read the Eternities."[1] The "objects" or "subjects" we allow to enter our minds reflect the spiritual competition we face on a daily basis. As "guardians" of our minds, we choose what thoughts to dwell on, what thoughts to discard, and what thoughts will bear fruit in our lives.

Proverbs 4:23 admonishes us to, "Keep thy heart with all diligence; for out of it are the issues of life." Proverbs 23:7 states, "As he thinketh in his heart, so is he." Proverbs 3:5–6 says, "Trust in the Lord with all thine heart; and lean not unto thine own understanding. In all thy ways acknowledge him, and he shall direct thy paths."

In the New Testament, the word *heart* originates from the Greek word, *kardia*. The heart is "the center and seat of spiritual life, the soul or mind is the fountain and seat of the thoughts, passions, desires, appetites, affections, purposes, endeavors…"[2] Biblically, heart refers to one's soul life or mind.

A person's soul is to be distinguished from the gift of holy spirit. The natural person consists of body and soul. Once the individual confesses and believes Romans 10:9–10, he or she becomes born again and is made up of body, soul, and spirit.[3]

James Allen, in *As a Man Thinketh*, writes "a man is literally what he thinks, his character being the complete sum of all his thoughts."[4] In the chapter, "Effect of Thought on Health and the Body," Allen links disease and health with our thought life.

> *Disease and health, like circumstances, are rooted in*
> *thought. Sickly thoughts will express themselves through*
> *a sickly body. Thoughts of fear have been known to kill*
> *a man as speedily as a bullet, and they are continually*

killing thousands of people just as surely though less
rapidly. The people who live in fear of disease are the
people who get it. Anxiety quickly demoralizes the whole
body, and lays it open to the entrance of disease; while
impure thoughts, even if not physically indulged, will
soon shatter the nervous system.
Strong, pure, and happy thoughts build up the body in
vigor and grace.
The body is a delicate and plastic instrument, which
responds readily to the thoughts by which it is impressed,
and habits of thought will produce their own effects, good
or bad, upon it.[5]

This chapter will focus on the connection between the mind and body, the power of believing, the influence of religion on health, the impact of emotions on the physical body, the power of thoughts, words, and actions, and the renewed mind state. How do our thoughts, emotions, words, and actions influence our physical health? What is the renewed mind? What are the obstacles that prevent us from renewing our minds to God's Word, and what are some practical keys to renewing our minds?

THE MIND AND BODY CONNECTION

René Descartes, the father of modern philosophy during the seventeenth century, posited the mind-body dualism; namely, that the mental and the physical are separate entities. In spite of this Cartesian dualism, there is a body of scientific and medical research that investigates the connection between the mind and emotions and their influence on the body. During the first half of the twentieth century, Walter Cannon and Hans Selye conducted research into the biology of stress and its relationship to our health.[6] The federal government's Integrated Neural Immune Program has spent sixteen million dollars on mind-body research, and many private foundations spend millions of dollars researching this topic.[7]

Nowhere is the connection between mind and body more evident than in the effects of stress on the body. Life is made up of all kinds of stressors such as raising children, caring for a sick relative, financial difficulties, poverty, unemployment, natural disasters, terrorist attacks, bad relationships, a demanding career, loneliness and isolation, dysfunctional families, divorce, and the death of loved ones. Stress can be positive or negative, involving the birth of a baby, the death of a child, preparation for a marriage, the dissolution of a marriage, the building of a home, or the relocation to a new home. Stress can be mental, emotional, physical, or spiritual. Stress is not something that merely happens to us, but rather, it is how we appraise and choose to respond to the situation at hand. What may be stressful to one individual may be regarded as a challenge to another. Witness, for example, the men and women who compete in the Olympic Games. As grueling as the training and preparations are, not many individuals would subject themselves to the physical, emotional, and mental pressures that come with competing in this world competition. How we respond to stress is dependent on many factors including our biological makeup, personality, past experiences, beliefs, education, physical health, and social environment. In the words of clinical psychologist Alex Zautra, stress is in the "eye of the beholder."[8]

Research suggests that the impact of chronic and prolonged stress may lead to impaired memory, a weakened immune system, high blood pressure, stomach ulcers, skin problems, digestive difficulties, stroke, heart attacks, premature aging, and in some cases, death. Ninety years ago, Walter Cannon, a Harvard physiologist, recognized that individuals who believed that a voodoo hex was placed on them by witch doctors could drop dead from an immediate and massive stress response.[9]

Herbert Benson writes in *The Mind/Body Effect* that "the success of such practices is dependent upon both the victim's awareness of the spell cast and the victim's strong adherence to his society's belief systems."[10] Voodoo or "hex" death has been documented since the sixteenth century in Africa, South America, the Caribbean, and Australia. There are certain basic features that characterize this phenomenon. First, the victim must be highly suggestible, with a strong belief in the power of the sorcerer or witch doctor who curses him or her. Second, once the curse is uttered, the victim has an attitude of helplessness and loses any will to live. A third characteristic is there is tremendous social pressure in that the victim's social world has the same belief system as the victim. Family and friends reinforce the negative belief of impending death by withdrawing and abandoning the victim to die in complete isolation. Interestingly, and not surprisingly, those who do not share this belief system, such as scientists, skeptics, and tourists, are not affected by the witch doctor's curse.[11]

THE BODY'S RESPONSE TO STRESS

What happens when the brain perceives a potential threat? The amygdala, a small almond-like structure located in the center of the brain, represents the fear system's command center. The amygdala is tied to other regions of the brain through nerve fibers. If the amygdala is activated, it doesn't wait for the conscious mind to respond but rather sends an immediate message to the hypothalamus, which then produces the hormone corticotropin, or CRF, which then signals the pituitary and adrenal glands. The bloodstream is then flooded with epinephrine or adrenaline, norepinephrine, and cortisol. These stress hormones shut down the digestive and immune system, and the body's resources are directed to fighting or fleeing. The heart rate increases, breathing quickens to take in more oxygen, the liver releases sugar into the blood for added energy, blood pressure rises, perspiration increases to regulate body temperature, stomach vessels constrict to force blood elsewhere, and extra blood is redirected to the arms and legs for energy.[12]

Harvard neurologist Martin Samuels maintains that "norepinephrine is toxic to tissues—probably all tissues, but in particular the heart." A month following the World Trade Center attack, patients with heart-related problems suffered life-threatening heart arrhythmias at more than twice the usual rate in New York City. Exposure to cortisol over an extended period of time can compromise the immune system and cause people to be more vulnerable to illnesses, diseases, and possibly cancer. Stress hormones also affect the brain and may even shrink the hippocampus, which plays an important role in processing and storing information.[13]

THE POWER OF BELIEVING

If there is a connection between the mind and body, what effect, if any, does believing have on the outcome of our health? The Bible is filled with examples of individuals receiving healing as a result of their believing.

Mathew 9:20–22 documents an incident where a woman "was diseased with an issue of blood" for twelve years. The woman believed that if she could touch the hem of Jesus's garment, she would be made whole. As a result of her believing, she was made whole in that very hour.

RENEWED MIND THE KEY TO POWER

Victor Paul Wierwille, in *The Bible Tells Me So*, writes that fear, worry, and anxiety represent negative believing. Negative believing is just as powerful as positive believing. Believing, whether positive or negative, will always bring to pass that which you believe. He writes:

> *The law of believing works equally effectively for both the sinner and the saint; however, the believer, because of the spirit from God within him, may bring forth more abundantly. If you doubt your recovery from sickness, you will by all means slow up and retard your own progress. Right believing is constantly knowing God's power and presence are in you and with you in every situation. How you think about the problem with which you are confronted at this very moment will determine the outcome. If you doubt its success, you have, by your own believing, determined its unsuccessful outcome.*
>
> *The evil of the world can never make you do evil or wrong unless you permit it through your own weakness of character or lack of believing.*
>
> *Once you start practicing the law of believing—right believing, believing God—you will find that the evil things that have been governing your life will soon fade away. God is always the victor over evil; but it is up to you to believe God and to make His will your will.* [14]

In *Christians Should be Prosperous,* Wierwille notes that "there is a close and definite relationship between the material and the spiritual realms. You just cannot separate the two, for they are inextricably bound by all the cords of life. The spiritual and material go hand in hand. Medical science in the field called psychosomatic medicine indicates that at least seventy to eighty percent of all diseases are rooted in the spiritual realm. The Bible clearly indicates that all material manifestations are the result of our spiritual attitude."[15]

Positive believing is the expectation of a positive outcome. If a person fails to study for an exam, however, no amount of positive believing will guarantee the individual will do well on a test. Taking the believing action to study diligently for the test, however, and then believing the outcome will be positive is a different story.

Believing, confessing, and acting on the promises of God's Word represents a higher level of believing than just believing positively. Believing and acting upon the Word of God is the unequivocal expectation of a spiritually advantageous outcome. It is having the confidence that what God has promised in His Word, He will absolutely bring to pass. Proverbs 3:26 states, "For the Lord shall be thy confidence, and shall keep thy foot from being taken." The psalmist writes that "it is better to trust in the Lord than to put confidence in man" (Psalm 118:8). Hebrews 10:35–36 encourages you to "cast not away therefore your confidence, which hath great recompense of reward. For ye have need of patience, that, after ye have done the will of God, ye might receive the promise."

Hebrews 10:38 states that "now the just shall live by faith [believing]: but if any man draw back, my soul shall have no pleasure in him." Hebrews 11:1 declares that "faith is the substance of things hoped for, the evidence of things not seen." The word *faith* comes from the Greek word *pistis* and is used 239 times in the New Testament. It means "steadfastness" and describes "him that believeth." Hebrews 11 documents several individuals in the Old Testament who had great faith or believing. Abel, Enoch, Noah,

Abraham, and Sara are recognized as great believers by God. They chose to believe in God and His Word rather than in their sense knowledge and the circumstances they were engulfed in.

RELIGION AND HEALTH

Dale Mathews is a medical doctor who believes in the importance of "whole person medicine." He cites, in *The Faith Factor,* a number of clinical studies which suggests that regular attendance at a church or synagogue is linked with better physical and mental health, greater life satisfaction, enhanced recovery from illness, and increased life expectancy.[16] The importance of combining a person's belief system with modern medicine is stressed as an important component to overall recovery, health and well-being.

Harold Koenig, Michael McCullough, and David Larson, in the *Handbook of Religion and Health,* document twelve hundred studies and four hundred research reviews of the twentieth century that examines the relationship between religion and a number of mental and physical health conditions. Some of the questions the authors examined were the influence of religion on health, the prevention of disease, and early detection. Research suggests that religious persons are more likely to live healthy lifestyles and are less likely to smoke and abuse alcohol, use illicit drugs, and engage in risky sexual behavior. There are some religious groups that have healthier diets and lower serum cholesterol levels and may even exercise more regularly than the general population. Furthermore, religious beliefs and behaviors may also be responsible for less depression and faster recovery from depression, improved coping with stress, greater well-being, and greater social support.[17]

In contrast, the authors also point out the deleterious effects that religious beliefs may have on health. There are adherents of some religious groups who may use religion to replace tradition-al medical care, who may fail to seek timely medical care, refuse blood transfusions, refuse to have their children immunized, re-fuse prenatal care and physician-assisted delivery of their children, and even promote, encourage, and foster child abuse.[18]

It appears that simply having faith is not as significant as *what a person chooses to believe*. Positive believing as well as negative believ-ing can be found in any church, mosque, synagogue, or ashram. What a person learns about the Bible, the nature of God, who Jesus Christ is, and the individual's role in the overall scheme of life has a great impact on the quality of life one chooses to live. Individuals who view God as a punishing deity who plagues people with health problems appear to suffer from worse mental health conditions than those who believe in a benevolent God. Once again, we choose our beliefs based upon what we are taught and what we choose to accept as truth. The potential benefits of religion, spirituality, and health appear to be important enough that in 1999, more than sixty medical schools in the United States offered courses on religion, spirituality, and medicine.[19]

EMOTIONS AND DISEASE

At the beginning of this chapter, we looked at the mind-body connection, the power of believing, and the influence of religion on health. We also looked at the influence of emotions, such as fear and its influence on individuals after the terrorist attack on the World Trade Center.

Don Colbert, in *Deadly Emotions,* reiterates the damaging effects that long-term stress and negative emotions have on the body.[20] Hostility, rage, and anger wreak havoc on a person's body and can lead to coronary disease, high blood pressure, gastrointestinal problems, rheumatoid arthritis, and death. Depression, worry, and negativity also impact a person's health and can lead to many disease-related illnesses.

Alex Zautra points out in *Emotions, Stress, and Health,* that "our responses to stressful events are the keys to successful adaptation." Resilience in dealing with negative experiences is the ability to recover or "bounce back" in the midst of coping with tremendous challenges in life. Resilient people have the ability "to retain perspective during stressful events."[21] In order to sustain themselves, resilient qualities need a community of emotional support and encouragement to be successful.

David Spiegel, a medical doctor, cites evidence that our resilience to stress, which includes disease-related distress, relates to how we as individuals handle our emotions. Coping with stress does not mean suppressing negative emotions, but rather, dealing with their negative effects. Furthermore, writing about past stressful experiences also results in symptoms being reduced in patients with asthma or rheumatoid arthritis.[22]

If medical research suggests there may be a connection between our minds and bodies, and that negative and unhealthy emotions may lead to certain disease-related illnesses, what impact do positive emotions have on a person's health? Proverbs 17:22 reminds us that "a merry heart doeth good like a medicine: but a broken spirit drieth the bones." The word *merry* is derived from the Hebrew word *sameach,* and it means "rejoicing." How do we acquire "merry" or rejoicing hearts in the midst of challenging circumstances? This topic is so provocative that *Time* magazine devoted its January 17, 2005, issue to "The Science of Happiness." Sonja Lyubomirsky, a California psychologist, provides us with "Eight Steps Toward a More Satisfying Life."[23] They include being thankful for your blessings, practicing acts of kindness, appreciating life's joys, being grateful to a mentor who guided you through life, practicing forgiveness, spending time with family and friends, taking care of your body by getting proper sleep and exercise, and cultivating strategies for coping with stress and hardships.

THE SPIRITUAL COMPETITION

The above steps are practical and useful suggestions to consider in cultivating happiness. No one would argue against the idea that eating properly, exercising, getting the right amount of rest, and being in a supportive family and social environment does wonders in providing a buffer against the pressures in life. However, Ephesians 6:12 warns us that "we wrestle not against flesh and blood, but against principalities, against powers, against the rulers of the darkness of this world, against spiritual wickedness in high places." We have a spiritual adversary who steals, kills, and destroys (John 10:10) and who walks about "as a roaring lion seeking whom he may devour" (1 Peter 5:8). "Wrestle" in Ephesians 6:12 is an athletic term and is used figuratively to highlight the spiritual competition we are engaged in.

The Amplified version of Ephesians 6:12 reads, "For we are not wrestling with flesh and blood [contending only with physical opponents], but against the despotisms, against the powers, against [the master spirits who are] the world rulers of this present darkness, against the spirit forces of wickedness in the heavenly (supernatural) sphere."

If our enemy is spiritual, and our conflict within this world is spiritual in nature, how do we protect ourselves and our loved ones from an opponent that we are unable to see, hear, taste, touch, or smell? From a biblical and spiritual perspective, the answer is to get born again and receive God's holy spirit. Once we learn how to operate the power of holy spirit by operating all nine manifestations, learn how to renew our minds to God's Word, and learn how to walk by the spirit and not by our senses, then we will be fully equipped to walk with victory.

In the Old Testament, the Israelites were not fully aware of the spiritual competition in life. They did not fully recognize that evil came from the Devil, a formidable spiritual opponent of the one true God. The following scriptures reflect this perspective:

I returned, and saw under the sun, that the race is not to the swift, nor the battle to the strong, neither yet bread to the wise, nor yet riches to men of understanding, nor yet favour to men of skill; but time and chance happeneth to them all.

For man also knoweth not his time: as the fishes that are taken in an evil net, and as the birds that are caught in the snare; so are the sons of men snared in an evil time, when it falleth suddenly upon them.
Ecclesiastes 9:11–12

The earth is given into the hand of the wicked: he covereth the faces of the judges thereof; if not, where, and who is he?
Job 9:24

In the New Testament, we recognize our spiritual adversary and what Jesus Christ came to accomplish: "He that committeth sin is of the devil; for the devil sinneth from the beginning. For this purpose the Son of God was manifested, that he might destroy the works of the devil" (1 John 3:8).

The spiritual competition, as discussed in chapter four, is a marathon and not a sprint. The crowns and rewards that we receive for our faithfulness in living by God's standards in this life are not measured by earthly treasures but by incorruptible treasures. As Paul wrote, "Eye hath not seen, nor ear heard, neither have entered into the heart of man, the things which God hath prepared for them that love him" (1 Corinthians 2:9).

The Bible is a rule book that guides and illuminates our path. God's Word makes us wiser than our spiritual adversary, the Devil.

> *For thou art my lamp, O Lord: and the Lord will lighten my darkness.*
> *For by thee I have run through a troop: by my God have I leaped over a wall.*
> *As for God, his way is perfect; the word of the Lord is tried; he is a buckler to all them that trust in him.*
> *For who is God, save the Lord? and who is a rock, save our God?*
> *God is my strength and power: and he maketh my way perfect.*
> *He maketh my feet like hinds' feet: and setteth me upon my high places.*
> 2 Samuel 22:29–34

> *O how love I thy law! It is my meditation all the day.*
> *Thou through thy commandments hast made me wiser than mine enemies: For they are ever with me.*
> Psalm 119:97–98

> *Thy word is a lamp unto my feet, and a light unto my path.*
> Psalm 119:105

The Bible helps us to successfully navigate the spiritual competition in life. Unlike an athletic competition, where a person signs up to play the game, by virtue of being born into this world, we are thrust into the spiritual competition. We may get pummeled by life or compete to win. Our spiritual adversary is formidable and seeks to annihilate and destroy people's lives.

Endurance, discipline and patience are required on the part of the believer.

Wherefore seeing we also are compassed about with so great a cloud of witnesses, let us lay aside every weight, and the sin which doth so easily beset us, and let us run with patience the race that is set before us.
Looking unto Jesus the author and finisher of our faith; who for the joy that was set before him endured the cross, despising the shame, and is set down at the right hand of the throne of God.
For consider him that endured such contradiction of sinners against himself, lest ye be wearied and faint in your minds.
Hebrews 12:1–3

Ephesians 6:10–19 and 1 Corinthians 12 describe the spiritual tools that are available to those who are born again of God's holy spirit. The gift of holy spirit was not made available until the day of Pentecost (Acts 2:1-4). It took the birth, life, death, resurrection, and ascension of Jesus Christ in order for God to make available this free gift to anyone who chooses to confess and believe Romans 10:9–10. God's will is that all should be saved and come unto the knowledge of the truth (1 Timothy 2:4). God never overrides free will but allows us to choose.

With humility, the Apostle Paul recognized his human limitations and the importance of relying on God.

And I, brethren, when I came to you, came not with excellency of speech or of wisdom, declaring unto you the testimony of God.
For I determined not to know any thing among you, save Jesus Christ, and him crucified.
And I was with you in weakness and in fear, and in much trembling.
And my speech and my preaching was not with enticing words of man's wisdom, but in demonstration of the Spirit and of power:
That your faith should not stand in the wisdom of men, but in the power of God.
Howbeit we speak wisdom among them that are perfect: yet not the wisdom of this world, nor of the princes of this world, that come to nought:
But we speak the wisdom of God in a mystery, even the hidden wisdom, which God ordained before the world unto our glory:
Which none of the princes of this world knew: for had they known it, they would not have crucified the Lord of glory.
1 Corinthians 2:1–8

Writing by revelation, Paul reveals an amazing truth. Had the "princes of this world" known that God would raise Jesus Christ from the dead, and with Christ's ascension the gift of holy spirit would be made available to anyone who believed, they never would have crucified God's only begotten Son. Now anyone who confesses and believes Romans 10:9–10 can be born again, receive eternal life, learn how to operate the gift of holy spirit with all nine manifestations, and walk with the same power that Jesus Christ walked with (John 14:12).

To whom God would make known what is the riches of the glory of this mystery among the Gentiles; which is Christ in you, the hope of glory.
Colossians 1:27

And ye are complete in him, which is the head of all principality and power:
In whom also ye are circumcised with the circumcision made without hands, in putting off the body of the sins of the flesh by the circumcision of Christ:
Buried with him in baptism, wherein also ye are risen with him through the faith of the operation of God, who hath raised him from the dead.
And you, being dead in your sins and the uncircumcision of your flesh, hath he quickened together with him, having forgiven you all trespasses;
Blotting out the handwriting of ordinances that was against us, and took it out of the way, nailing it to his cross;
And having spoiled principalities and powers, he made a shew of them openly, triumphing over them in it.
Colossians 2:10–15

THE RENEWED MIND WALK

The renewed mind is the ability to align our thoughts to the Word of God in spite of emotions and circumstances that pull our minds to the senses realm. Chapter five dealt with the conflict between sense knowledge and spiritual knowledge. Examples were given of people who walked by their senses and those who walked with spiritual knowledge. The five senses are an important means of ascertaining and processing information about the world we live in. However, when we are born again of holy spirit, we have access to a higher realm of knowledge, which is spiritual in nature. Learning how to walk by the spirit and not by our senses takes time, patience, and endurance. It requires humility and discipline to track our minds and actions with the Word of God rather than react to circumstances with our emotions.

THE RENEWED MIND CHALLENGE

Because the Devil is the god of this world (2 Corinthians 4:4), he is a master at manipulating the environment. The challenges we face today are no different than they were in the past. "There is no new thing under the sun," Ecclesiastes 1:9 declares. We may not always be able to control the circumstances or the attacks in our lives, but we do have the ability to determine our responses to the mental, physical, emotional, and spiritual challenges that we face on a daily basis.

Just as nutrition and exercise, or a lack thereof, affect our physical bodies, what we feed our minds impacts our spiritual health. "For they that are after the flesh do mind the things of the flesh; But they that are after the Spirit the things of the Spirit. For to be carnally minded is death; but to be spiritually minded is life and peace. Because the carnal mind is enmity against God: for it is not subject to the law of God, neither indeed can be. So then they that are in the flesh cannot please God" (Romans 8:5–8).

There is an important distinction between being carnally minded and being spiritually minded. The carnal mind ultimately leads to destruction and death, while the spiritual mind leads to life and peace. Being carnally minded is characterized by being dominated by things of the flesh or the five senses. Succumbing to the "lust of the flesh, and the lust of the eyes, and the pride of life is not of the Father, but is of the world" (1 John 2:16). We have the freedom to choose to be masters or slaves to our thoughts and emotions.

Walking by the Spirit

When we are born again of God's holy spirit, we receive eternal life. Our minds, however, are not suddenly transformed to think godly thoughts. We still have an "old man nature" we must contend with on a daily basis. The old man nature represents our habit patterns and thoughts before we had an accurate knowledge of God's Word. Spiritually, our old man nature is rendered dead. However, we must decide to keep him dead by renewing our minds to believe and act on God's Word.

Knowing this, that our old man is crucified with him, that the body of sin might be destroyed, that henceforth we should not serve sin.
Romans 6:6

That ye put off concerning the former conversation the old man, which is corrupt according to the deceitful lusts; And be renewed in the spirit of your mind; And that ye put on the new man, which after God is created in righteousness and true holiness.
Ephesians 4:22–24

But now ye also put off all these; anger, wrath, malice, blasphemy, filthy communication out of your mouth. Lie not one to another, seeing that ye have put off the old man with his deeds;

And have put on the new man, which is renewed in
knowledge after the image of him that created him.
Colossians 3:8–10

We decide to put off the old man habit patterns and put on the new spiritual man. ("Man," in the spiritual context, includes both genders.) Walking by the spirit involves renewing our minds to God's Word on a moment by moment basis. We are to put on the mind of Christ.

Renewing our minds begins with a personal decision to read the Word of God daily, retain and memorize scriptures, allow the engrafted Word to dwell deeply within our hearts, and then believe, confess, and act on the promises of God. "Finally, brethren, whatsoever things are true, whatsoever things are honest, whatsoever things are just, whatsoever things are pure, whatsoever things are lovely, whatsoever things are of good report; if there be any virtue, and if there be any praise, think on these things" (Philippians 4:8).

Philippians 2:5 encourages us to "Let this mind be in you, which was also in Christ Jesus." We choose to think, confess, and do the Word of God. God lovingly gave us His Word so we would not be ensnared by Satan's devices. As parents desire to protect their children from evil, so God has given us His written Word to warn us about the destructive evil in the ways of the world. In Deuteronomy, Moses presented two options to the Israelites: "I call heaven and earth to record this day against you, that I have set before you life and death, blessing and cursing: therefore choose life, that both thou and thy seed may live: That thou mayest love the Lord thy God, and that thou mayest obey his voice, and that thou mayest cleave unto him: for he is thy life, and the length of thy days: that thou mayest dwell in the land which the Lord sware unto thy fathers, to Abraham, to Isaac, and to Jacob, to give them" (Deuteronomy 30: 19–20).

God's desire is that we choose life and all the blessings that come from living His Word. Colossians 3:16 encourages us to "Let the Word of Christ dwell in you richly in all wisdom; teaching and admonishing one another in psalms and hymns and spiritual songs, singing with grace in your hearts to the Lord." Rather than being a victim of life, we can be victorious by responding with the Word of God, "It is written," to all of life's challenges.

Meditating or reflecting deeply upon the greatness of God's Word brings tremendous blessings to our lives. "Blessed is the man that walketh not in the counsel of the ungodly, nor standeth in the way of sinners, nor sitteth in the seat of the scornful. But his delight is in the law of the Lord; and in his law doth he meditate day and night. And he shall be like a tree planted by the rivers of water, that bringeth forth his fruit in his season; his leaf also shall not wither; and whatsoever he doeth shall prosper" (Psalms 1:1–3). God's Word, when believed, is like a healing balm to your soul.

All of us have faults that we may or may not be consciously aware of. As we read the Bible with an attitude of humility, the light from God's Word exposes those areas in our lives that need to be corrected. God's Word has the answer to any challenge that we may face in life.

Change occurs when we decide to live our lives according to the integrity of God's Word, to the best of our abilities. God knows we are not perfect. God does not ask for perfection, but asks that we be faithful to His Word. "A faithful man shall abound with blessings," Proverbs 28:20 declares.

King David, a man after God's own heart, recognized the importance of seeking God's will rather than following his own will. He demonstrated great humility when he sought God to "cleanse thou me from secret faults" (Psalm 19:12). With meekness, David asked God to "create in me a clean heart, O God; and renew a right spirit within me" (Psalm 51:10). David's humility is further expressed in Psalm 139:23–24: "Search me, O God, and know my heart: try me, and know my thoughts: And see if there be any wicked way in me, and lead me in the way everlasting." David endeavored to align his will with God's will rather than compromise God's Word to justify his weaknesses. Psalm 143:10 demonstrates this truth: "Teach me to do thy will; for thou art my God: thy spirit is good; lead me into the land of uprightness."

With an attitude of humility, the psalmist wrote the following:

> *With my whole heart have I sought thee: O let me not wander from thy commandments.*
> *Thy word have I hid in mine heart, that I might not sin against thee.*
> Psalm 119:10–11

> *I will delight myself in thy statutes: I will not forget thy word.*
> Psalm 119:16

When learning the standard of God's Word, conflicts may arise between decisions that were made in the past and godly decisions that should be made in the present. The Apostle Paul experienced this conflict when he wrote, "For the good that I would I do not: but the evil which I would not, that I do. Now if I do that I would not, it is no more I that do it, but sin that dwelleth in me. I thank God through Jesus Christ our Lord. So then with the mind I myself serve the law of God; but with the flesh the law of sin" (Romans 7:19–20, 25).

What do we do when our thoughts are contrary to the Word of God? "Casting down imaginations, and every high thing that exalteth itself against the knowledge of God, and bringing into captivity every thought to the obedience of Christ" (2 Corinthians 10:5). We are to cast down those thoughts that are contrary to God's Word and replace those thoughts with the Word of God.

Our brains process millions of messages a day. We choose what thoughts to focus on, what thoughts to discard, and what thoughts to bring into fruition. Focused thinking on God's Word yields positive results, while unfocused thinking yields confusion. James 1:8 states that "a double minded man is unstable in all his ways." The word *double-minded* means "vacillating in opinion or purpose." God does not want us to be double-minded but we are to focus our thoughts on His Word.

Jesus Christ taught about the power of thoughts that come from within.

> *O generation of vipers, how can ye, being evil, speak good things? for out of the abundance of the heart the mouth speaketh.*
> *A good man out of the good treasure of the heart bringeth forth good things: and an evil man out of the evil treasure bringeth forth evil things.*
> Mathew 12:34–35

> *There is nothing from without a man, that entering in him can defile him: but the things which come out of him, those are they that defile the man.*
> Mark 7:15

And he said, That which cometh out of the man, that
defileth the man.
For from within, out of the heart of men, proceed evil
thoughts, adulteries, fornications, murders,
Thefts, covetousness, wickedness, deceit, lasciviousness,
an evil eye, blasphemy, pride, foolishness:
All these evil things come from within, and defile the
man.
Mark 7:20–23

Thinking and acting on godly thoughts yields positive results. James Allen writes, "A man cannot directly choose his circumstances, but he can choose his thoughts, and so indirectly, yet surely, shape his circumstances."[24]

THE POWER OF WORDS

In addition to aligning our thoughts to God's Word, our confessions, or the words that we speak, will also yield specific results. If we are to see the power of God operate in our lives, our words must track with our thoughts that are Word-based. Proverbs 18:21 emphasizes the importance of the words that we speak: "Death and life are in the power of the tongue: and they that love it shall eat the fruit thereof." Like our thoughts, the words we speak can be positive or negative. I once knew a woman who continually confessed that she would come down with cancer. Eventually, she was stricken with cancer.

The power of the tongue yields encouragement or criticism, love or hate, health or sickness, strength or weakness, joy or misery. The power of the tongue is described in the book of James:

Even so the tongue is a little member, and boasteth great
things. Behold, how great a matter a little fire kindleth!
And the tongue is a fire, a world of iniquity: so is the
tongue among our members, that it defileth the whole
body, and setteth on fire the course of nature; and it is set
on fire of hell.
For every kind of beasts, and of birds, and of serpents,
and of things in the sea, is tamed, and hath been tamed of
mankind:
But the tongue can no man tame; it is an unruly evil,
full of deadly poison.
Therewith bless we God, even the Father; and therewith
curse we men, which are made after the similitude of
God.
Out of the same mouth proceedeth blessing and cursing.
My brethren, these things ought not so to be.
James 3:5–10

A description of the power of words and their effects on
people's lives is also found in the book of Job. As described in
chapter three, Job is a story about a godly man who endured great
mental, emotional, and physical suffering as a result of horrendous
attacks by the Devil. He lost his children, livestock, and servants.
Rather than being comforters and encouragers during this period
of great distress, Job's friends are described by him as "forgers of
lies, physicians of no value," and "miserable comforters" (Job 13:4,
16:2). With cutting and accusatory words, Job's friends chastised
and accused him of some transgression that may have been done
in the past. They implied that somehow Job was responsible for
the evil that had befallen his family. The destructive nature of his
friends' words was expressed by Job when he said, "How long will

ye vex my soul, and break me in pieces with words?" (Job 19:2). The word *vex* is derived from the Hebrew word, *yagah,* and it means "to afflict or grieve one's soul."

Like Job, many of us have experienced words of negativity and criticism at some point in our lives. Negative words can cut to the core of our souls and are a form of harassing evil. It takes discipline and a renewed mind to recognize where the fiery darts are coming from and to stand and withstand these attacks.

Proverbs describes the words of a fool and a talebearer.

> *A fool's lips enter into contention, and his mouth calleth*
> *for strokes.*
> *A fool's mouth is his destruction, and his lips are the*
> *snare of his soul.*
> *The words of a talebearer are as wounds, and they go*
> *down into the innermost parts of the belly.*
> Proverbs 18:6–8

> *He that goeth about as a talebearer revealeth secrets:*
> *therefore meddle not with him that flattereth with his lips.*
> Proverbs 20:19

In contrast, "Whoso keepeth his mouth and his tongue keepeth his soul from troubles" (Proverbs 21:23).

The Bible points out the power of words and the consequences of false flattery from the mouth of an adulterous woman: "To keep thee from the evil woman, from the flattery of the tongue of a strange woman. Lust not after her beauty in thine heart; neither let her take thee with her eyelids. For by means of a whorish woman a man is brought to a piece of bread: and the adulteress will hunt for the precious life" (Proverbs 6:24–26).

The following passage describes six things that God hates, and seven are an abomination to Him: "A proud look, a lying tongue, and hands that shed innocent blood, An heart that deviseth wicked imaginations, feet that be swift in running to mischief [evil], A false witness that speaketh lies, and he that soweth discord among brethren" (Proverbs 6:16–19).

Psalm 52:2–4 records the power of the tongue to work deceitfully and to devise evil with "devouring words." Paul warned the believers in Rome of individuals who were causing division in the church: "Now I beseech you, brethren, mark them which cause divisions and offences contrary to the doctrine which ye have learned; and avoid them. For they that are such serve not our Lord Jesus Christ, but their own belly; and by good words and fair speeches deceive the hearts of the simple" (Romans 16:17–18). "Good words and fair speeches" can deceive innocent people by pulling them away from the standard of the written Word.

The Bible is filled with examples of how words can be used for good or evil, and emphasizes the importance of using wisdom when choosing our words:

> *Thy tongue deviseth mischiefs; like a sharp razor, working deceitfully.*
> *Thou lovest evil more than good; and lying rather than to speak righteousness. Selah.*
> *Thou lovest all devouring words, O thou deceitful tongue.*
> Psalms 52:2–4

> *The words of the wicked are to lie in wait for blood: but the mouth of the upright shall deliver them.*
> Proverbs 12:6

A man hath joy by the answer of his mouth: and a word
spoken in due season, how good is it!
Proverbs 15:23

The thoughts of the wicked are an abomination to the
Lord: But the words of the pure are pleasant words.
Proverbs 15:26

Pleasant words are as an honeycomb, sweet to the soul,
and health to the bones.
Proverbs 16:24

Keep thy tongue from evil, and thy lips from speaking
guile.
Psalm 34:13

He that hath knowledge spareth his words: and a man of
understanding is of an excellent spirit.
Even a fool, when he holdeth his peace, is counted
wise: and he that shutteth his lips is esteemed a man of
understanding.
Proverbs 17:27–28

The Bible provides wisdom regarding the power that words
have over the listener. In the heat of anger, we may be tempted
to say things we may later regret. The psalmist provides a remedy for this in the following passage: "A soft answer turneth
away wrath: but grievous words stir up anger. The tongue of
the wise useth knowledge aright: but the mouth of fools po-
ureth out foolishness...A wholesome tongue is a tree of life:

but perverseness therein is a breach in the spirit" (Proverbs 15:1–2, 4).

Additional references on the power of words are found in the following scriptures:

A word fitly spoken is like apples of gold in pictures of silver.
Proverbs 25:11

Whoso keepeth his mouth and his tongue keepeth his soul from troubles.
Proverbs 21:23

Let no corrupt communication proceed out of your mouth, but that which is good to the use of edifying, that it may minister grace unto the hearers.
Ephesians 4:29

Jesus Christ encouraged his disciples to abide in the words that he spoke, so that their joy would be complete:

If ye abide in me, and my words abide in you, ye shall ask what ye will, and it shall be done unto you.
Herein is my Father glorified, that ye bear much fruit; so shall ye be my disciples.
As the Father hath loved me, so have I loved you: continue ye in my love.
If ye keep my commandments, ye shall abide in my love; even as I have kept my Father's commandments, and abide in his love.

These things have I spoken unto you, that my joy
might remain in you, and that your joy might be full
[complete].
John 15:7–11

The word *disciples*, in verse 8, is the Greek word *mathetes,* and it means "taught or trained one." As we learn to track our thoughts, words, and actions with the written Word, we become disciples in doing the works of Jesus Christ (John 8:31–32, John 14:12).

THE POWER OF ACTION

Thoughts and words are insufficient, if they fail to produce godly action. Proverbs 20:11 states that "even a child is known by his doings, whether his work be pure, and whether it be right." The book of Acts records the early Christians putting the teachings of Jesus Christ into practice. In spite of experiencing religious persecution, the disciples shared God's Word, walked with the power of God, and brought great mental, physical, and spiritual deliverance to others.

The book of James emphasizes the importance of being "doers of the Word:"

Wherefore lay apart all filthiness and superfluity of
naughtiness, and receive with meekness the engrafted
word, which is able to save your souls.
But be ye doers of the word, and not hearers only,
deceiving your own selves.
For if any be a hearer of the word, and not a doer, he is
like unto a man beholding his natural face in a glass:
For he beholdeth himself, and goeth his way, and
straightway forgetteth what manner of man he was.

But whoso looketh into the perfect law of liberty, and
continueth therein, he being not a forgetful hearer, but a
doer of the work, this man shall be blessed in his deed.
James 1:21–25

James exhorted the believers to put aside all filthiness, evil, and wicked ways and to receive, with humility, the "engrafted" Word that saves peoples' souls.

Although we are saved by grace and not by works, we prove our faith or believing by our works (Ephesians 2:8–9, Romans 3:24, Galatians 2:16).

What doth it profit, my brethren, though a man say he
hath faith, and have not works? can faith save him?
If a brother or sister be naked, and destitute of daily food,
And one of you say unto them, Depart in peace, be ye
warmed and filled; notwithstanding ye give them not those
things which are needful to the body; what doth it profit?
Even so faith, if it hath not works, is dead, being alone.
Yea, a man may say, Thou hast faith, and I have works:
shew me thy faith without thy works, and I will shew
thee my faith by my works.
For as the body without the spirit is dead, so faith without
works is dead also.
James 2:14–18, 26

In Acts 2:4, the disciples, having received the gift of holy spirit on the day of Pentecost, put their faith into action by speaking God's Word and bringing deliverance to the lives of others. In Acts 9, we read of Ananias being called by God to minister to Saul, a persecutor of the church (Acts 9:10–18). Saul, who later became known as the Apostle Paul, got born again and preached Christ in the synagogues, teaching that Jesus was the Son of God (Acts 9:20). In the same chapter, we also read of a man who was sick of the palsy for eight years, who was healed (Acts 9:33–34), and we read of a miracle performed when Peter raised Tabitha from the dead (Acts 9:40).

By utilizing the power of holy spirit, and believing and acting on God's Word, many miracles, signs, and wonders were performed in the name of Jesus Christ. In Acts 14:8, Paul ministered to a man at Lystra who was crippled from his mother's womb, who then "leaped and walked."

OBSTACLES TO THE RENEWED MIND

A number of obstacles may prevent us from renewing our minds to God's Word. The following list describes what may impede us from walking with the renewed mind, fully operating the gift of holy spirit, and manifesting the power of God.

Ignorance of God's Word

If we do not know what is available from the Bible, it is difficult to appropriate the promises and blessings from God. Romans 10:17 states that "faith cometh by hearing, and hearing by the word of God." Hosea 4:6 declares, "My people are destroyed for lack of knowledge: because thou hast rejected knowledge, I will also reject thee ..." The word *destroyed* in this record comes from the Hebrew word *damah,* and it means "to be cut off." In contrast to not knowing the Word of God, Psalm 107:20 proclaims, "He sent his word, and healed them, and delivered them from their destructions." Ignorance is not an excuse for not knowing or learning the Bible. Research, teaching, and Bible fellowships are readily available to those who genuinely want to know, learn, and apply the greatness of God's Word in their lives.

Pride

Proverbs 29:23 states that "a man's pride shall bring him low: but honour shall uphold the humble in spirit." The Bible teaches us not to trust in ourselves but in God and His Word. "He that trusteth in his own heart is a fool: but whoso walketh wisely, he shall be delivered" (Proverbs 28:26). Men and women who walk for God recognize that it is God who works within them "both to will and to do of his good pleasure" (Philippians 2:13).

And such trust have we through Christ to God-ward:
Not that we are sufficient of ourselves to think any thing
as of ourselves; but our sufficiency is of God.
2 Corinthians 3:4–5

For God, who commanded the light to shine out of
darkness, hath shined in our hearts, to give the light of the
knowledge of the glory of God in the face of Jesus Christ.
But we have this treasure in earthen vessels, that the
excellency of the power may be of God, and not of us.
2 Corinthians 4:6–7

Wherefore he saith, God resisteth the proud, but giveth
grace unto the humble.
Submit yourselves therefore to God. Resist the devil, and
he will flee from you.
Draw nigh to God, and he will draw nigh to you.
James 4:6–8

By humility and the fear [respect] of the Lord are riches,
and honour, and life.
Proverbs 22:4

Rebellion

Rebellion against God and His Word prevents an individual from claiming the promises in the Bible. 1 Samuel 15:23 states, "For rebellion is as the sin of witchcraft, and stubbornness is as iniquity and idolatry." Lucifer was the first angel who rebelled against God. Not only was he filled with pride, egotism, and rebellion, but he desired to be worshipped like the one true God (Isaiah 14:12–14). Ultimately, he "shalt be brought down to hell, to the sides of the pit" (Isaiah 14:15).

Even the Israelites, whom Moses led out of Egypt, rebelled against God.

> *They forgot God their saviour, which had done great
> things in Egypt;*
> *Wondrous works in the land of Ham, and terrible things
> by the Red sea.*
> *Therefore he said that he would destroy them, had not
> Moses his chosen stood before him in the breach, to turn
> away his wrath, lest he should destroy them.*
> *Yea, they despised the pleasant land, they believed not his
> word:*
> *But murmured in their tents, and hearkened not unto the
> voice of the Lord.*
> *Therefore he lifted up his hand against them, to
> overthrow them in the wilderness:*
> *To overthrow their seed also among the nations, and to
> scatter them in the lands.*
> *They joined themselves also unto Baalpeor, and ate the
> sacrifices of the dead.*
> Psalm 106:21–28

Sin Consciousness

Sin consciousness refers to not knowing and claiming what Jesus Christ accomplished for us by cleansing us of all sins.[25] As a result of Jesus Christ's life, death, resurrection, and ascension, we can live more than abundant lives without any sense of sin, guilt, or condemnation.

> *For this is my blood of the new testament, which is shed*
> *for many for the remission of sins.*
> Mathew 26:28

> *Therefore we are buried with him by baptism into death:*
> *that like as Christ was raised up from the dead by the*
> *glory of the Father, even so we also should walk in*
> *newness of life.*
> *For if we have been planted together in the likeness of his*
> *death, we shall be also in the likeness of his resurrection:*
> *Knowing this, that our old man is crucified with him,*
> *that the body of sin might be destroyed, that henceforth we*
> *should not serve sin.*
> Romans 6:4–6

> *Knowing that Christ being raised from the dead dieth no*
> *more; death hath no more dominion over him.*
> *For in that he died, he died unto sin once: but in that he*
> *liveth, he liveth unto God.*
> *Likewise reckon ye also yourselves to be dead indeed unto*
> *sin, but alive unto God through Jesus Christ our Lord.*
> *Let not sin therefore reign in your mortal body, that ye*
> *should obey it in the lusts thereof.*

Neither yield ye your members as instruments of
unrighteousness unto sin: but yield yourselves unto God,
as those that are alive from the dead, and your members as
instruments of righteousness unto God.
For sin shall not have dominion over you: for ye are not
under the law, but under grace.
Romans 6:9–14

Christ hath redeemed us from the curse of the law, being
made a curse for us: for it is written,
Cursed is everyone that hangeth on a tree.
Galatians 3:13

Having this freedom in Christ does not give us license to sin and to "frustrate the grace of God" (Galatians 2:21). But rather, having been made free from sin, we "became the servants of righteousness" (Romans 6:18).

But now being made free from sin, and become servants
to God, ye have your fruit unto holiness, and the end
everlasting life.
For the wages of sin is death; but the gift of God is
eternal life through Jesus Christ our Lord.
Romans 6:22–23

But Christ being come an high priest of good things to
come, by a greater and more perfect tabernacle, not made
with hands, that is to say, not of this building;

Neither by the blood of goats and calves, but by his
own blood he entered in once into the holy place, having
obtained eternal redemption for us.
Hebrews 9:11–12

For the scripture saith, Whosoever believeth on him shall
not be ashamed.
For there is no difference between the Jew [Judean] and
the Greek: for the same Lord over all is rich unto all that
call upon him.
For whosoever shall call upon the name of the Lord shall
be saved.
Romans 10:11–13

Curious Arts

Ultimately, everything is spiritual in nature. The physical is a manifestation of the spiritual. If objects are an extension of thoughts, then everything gives off something, be it positive or negative. The Bible is very clear in condemning the practices of sorcerers, enchanters, astrologers, and witches (Leviticus 19:31, Leviticus 20:6, Leviticus 20:27, Isaiah 8:19-20, Isaiah 47:9-15, Isaiah 57:3, Micah 5:12, Nahum 3:4–5, Malachi 3:5).

And the rest of the men which were not killed by these
plagues yet repented not of the works of their hands, that
they should not worship devils, and idols of gold, and
silver, and brass, and stone and of wood: which neither
can see, nor hear, nor walk:

*Neither repented they of their murders, nor of their
sorceries, nor of their fornication; nor of their thefts.*
Revelation 9:20–21

*Now the works of the flesh are manifest, which are these;
Adultery, fornication, uncleanness, lasciviousness,
Idolatry, witchcraft, hatred, variance, emulations, wrath,
strife, seditions, heresies,
Envyings, murders, drunkenness, revellings, and such
like; of the which I tell you before, as I have also told you
in time past, that they which do such things shall not
inherit the kingdom of God.*
Galatians 5:19–21

Renouncing "curious arts," or books dealing with the occult, was critical to the successful movement of God's Word in
the first-century Church. "Many of them also which used curious arts brought their books together, and burned them before
all men: and they counted the price of them, and found it fifty
thousand pieces of silver. So mightily grew the word of God and
prevailed" (Acts 19:19–20).

The spiritual devices of the Devil are subtle and extensive.
"Evil men and seducers shall wax worse and worse, deceiving, and
being deceived" (2 Timothy 3:13). Following the second session
of a Bible class that I enrolled in, God began to show me what
I needed to remove in my home that was causing me to be un-
peaceful. I threw away books, artwork, and objects dealing with
spiritualism, psychic phenomena, and the occult. To this day, I am
spiritually vigilant of what is brought into my home. I ask myself,
does this object remind me of God's beauty, peace, and harmony,
or does it evoke feelings of negativity, darkness, and idolatry?

Eliminating the following items will bring peace in your life so you can begin to focus on the promises in God's Word: books, music, artwork, movies, video games, idols, and objects dealing with or advocating suicide, drugs, rampant sexuality, violence and death, the New Age, astrology, amulets, astral projection, automatic writing, channeling, clairvoyance, the occult, séances, spirit guides, psychic phenomena, sorcery, crystal balls, extrasensory perception, telekinesis, fire walking, fortune-telling, numerology, games such as the Ouija board and tarot cards, palm reading, parapsychology, past life regression, psychic healing, rebirthing, reincarnation, Satanism, devil worship, voodoo, white and black witchcraft.[26] Removing these items, activities, and associations from your life may not be an easy task, but it can be done. With prayer, the support and prayers of a community of believers, the gift of holy spirit, and by God's grace and mercy, deliverance is available to anyone who truly wants it.

Slothfulness

In our society, some people want something for nothing. There is a price for everything. The only genuinely free gift that was ever made available to humankind was the gift of eternal life. However, even this had a price. It took the innocent blood of Jesus Christ, who freely gave his life for all, so that anyone who wants the gift of holy spirit can receive eternal life. "For God so loved the world, that he gave his only begotten Son, that whosoever believeth in him should not perish, but have everlasting life" (John 3:16).

Slothfulness refers to laziness and indolence. However, in a figurative sense in the Old and the New Testaments, there is a deeper spiritual meaning. Proverbs 19:15 states that "slothfulness casteth into a deep sleep; and an idle soul shall suffer hunger." In this context, slothfulness refers to mental inertia or spiritual dullness. Paul refers to this spiritual slumber in Ephesians 5:14: "Wherefore he saith, Awake thou that sleepest, and arise from the dead, and Christ shall give thee light."

Prior to learning the Word of God, I was in a mental stupor or a spiritually comatose state. When I began learning and reading the Bible, my eyes of understanding began to be spiritually enlightened. God's Word and the gift of holy spirit literally enlightened my eyes of understanding to see things from a spiritual point of view.

In the following scriptures, Paul warns the Galatians against turning back to their old habit patterns of thinking. The Judeans, who were born again, were tempted to turn back to living their lives according to the Mosaic law rather than in the freedom inherent in the gospel of Jesus Christ.

> *But now, after that ye have known God, or rather are*
> *known of God, how turn ye again to the weak and*
> *beggarly elements, whereunto ye desire again to be in*
> *bondage?*
> Galatians 4:9

> *Stand fast therefore in the liberty wherewith Christ hath made*
> *us free, and be not entangled again with the yoke of bondage.*
> Galatians 5:1

> *For in Jesus Christ neither circumcision availeth*
> *anything, nor uncircumcision; but faith which worketh*
> *by love.*
> *Ye did run well; who did hinder you that ye should not*
> *obey the truth?*
> Galatians 5:6–7

Jesus Christ taught in John 8:31 that "if you continue in my Word then are ye my disciples indeed." The word *continue* comes from the Greek word *menō,* and it means "to remain." Like the Galatians, the Christian today is encouraged to remain spiritually awake in God's Word. We are to remember what Christ accomplished for us and not return to the bondage of the law or to the religious traditions and rituals that prevent us from claiming all that is available as sons and daughters of the living God.

But ye, brethren, are not in darkness, that that day should overtake you as a thief.
Ye are all the children of light, and the children of the day: we are not of the night, nor of darkness.
Therefore let us not sleep, as do others; but let us watch and be sober.
1 Thessalonians 5:4–6

Love worketh no ill to his neighbor: therefore love is the fulfilling of the law.
And that, knowing the time that now it is high time to awake out of sleep: for now is our salvation nearer than when we believed.
The night is far spent, the day is at hand: let us therefore cast off the works of darkness, and let us put on the armor of light.
Romans 13:10–12

Negativity and Unbelief
Additional stumbling blocks that impede us from renewing our minds to God's Word are negativity and unbelief. The Bible is

filled with examples of individuals whom Jesus Christ confronted because of their negativity and unbelief. In the following passage, Jesus confronted the religious leaders who held their traditions above the law of Moses:

> *Then came to Jesus scribes and Pharisees, which were of*
> *Jerusalem, saying,*
> *Why do thy disciples transgress the tradition of the elders?*
> *For they wash not their hands when they eat bread.*
> *But he answered and said unto them, Why do ye also*
> *transgress the commandment of God by your tradition?*
> *For God commanded, saying, Honour thy father and*
> *mother: and, He that curseth father or mother, let him die*
> *the death.*
> *But ye say, Whosoever shall say to his father or his*
> *mother, It is a gift, by whatsoever thou mightest be*
> *profited by me;*
> *And honour not his father or his mother, he shall be free.*
> *Thus have ye made the commandment of God of none*
> *effect by your tradition.*
> Mathew 15:1–6

With great boldness and confidence, Jesus confronted the scribes and the Pharisees with God's Word. Jesus's response to the religious leaders' criticism about eating with publicans and sinners (Mark 2:17), healing a man with a withered hand on the sabbath day (Mark 3:1–5), or being tempted by the Devil in the wilderness (Luke 4:1–12) was always with the Word of God, "It is written." The religious leaders' criticism, negativity, and unbelief did not prevent Jesus from doing what God called him to do.

In some instances, Jesus removed the presence of negative and unbelieving people prior to performing a healing. In Mark 5:23, Jesus was approached by a father imploring him to heal his daughter, who was "at the point of death." Upon arriving at the home of the ruler of the synagogue, he was met with much weeping and wailing by the people.

> *And when he was come in, he saith unto them, Why make ye this ado, and weep? The damsel is not dead, but sleepeth.*
> *And they laughed him to scorn. But when he had put them all out, he taketh the father and the mother of the damsel, and them that were with him, and entereth in where the damsel was lying.*
> *And he took the damsel by the hand, and said unto her, Talitha cumi; which is, being interpreted, Damsel, I say unto thee, arise.*
> *And straightway the damsel arose, and walked; for she was of the age of twelve years. And they were astonished with a great astonishment.*
> *And he charged them straitly that no man should know it; and commanded that something should be given her to eat.*
> Mark 5:39–43

In order to perform a miracle, believing, on the part of the parent or the recipient, must be present. "But without faith [believing] it is impossible to please him: for he that cometh to God must believe that he is, and that he is a rewarder of them that diligently seek him" (Hebrews 11:6).

Those who questioned Jesus's lineage and chose not to believe that he was the Son of God did not fully experience the deliverance that was available from God. Mathew 13:54–58 and Mark 6:1–6 documents the skepticism and unbelief of the people in his own country when Jesus taught in the synagogue. People were astonished by his wisdom and mighty works and immediately sought to put him in his place by reminding Jesus that he was a carpenter's son, with brothers and sisters (Mathew 13:54–56). Mathew 13:57–58 says they were offended by Jesus, and as a consequence, "he did not many mighty works there because of their unbelief."

A SPIRITUAL DIET FOR
THE RENEWED MIND

What we feed our minds on a daily basis has a direct impact on the quality of our spiritual lives. Just as a daily diet of junk food will eventually lead to health problems, positive or negative thoughts that we feed our minds will eventually yield specific results. Thoughts of doubt, worry, and fear will inevitably lead to anxiety, negativity, and mental distress. The effects of negative thoughts and emotions on our mental, physical, and emotional well-being have been documented in this chapter.

The renewed mind involves disciplining and controlling our thinking to think God's Word instead of negative thoughts that seek to dominate our minds. The field of cognitive-behavioral psychology provides a model that maintains that our thoughts influence our emotions and behavior.[27] As we substitute our negative thoughts and meditate or think deeply about the Word of God, there are mental, physical, emotional, and spiritual benefits that come from believing, confessing, and applying the principles from the Bible.

What follows are some of my favorite scriptures that help me to renew my mind when circumstances and mental pressure try to pull me in the opposite direction.

Trusting God

*Trust in the Lord with all thine heart; and lean not unto
thine own understanding.
In all thy ways acknowledge him, and he shall direct thy
paths.*
Proverbs 3:5–6

*Trust in the Lord, and do good; so shalt thou dwell in the
land, and verily thou shalt be fed.
Delight thyself also in the Lord; and he shall give thee the
desires of thine heart.
Commit thy way unto the Lord; trust also in him; and
he shall bring it to pass.
And he shall bring forth thy righteousness as the light,
and thy judgment as the noonday.*
Psalm 37: 3–6

*And the Lord shall help them, and deliver them: he shall
deliver them from the wicked, and save them, because
they trust in him.*
Psalm 37:40

*But it is good for me to draw near to God: I have put my
trust in the Lord God, that I may declare all thy works.*
Psalm 73:28

*Every word of God is pure: he is a shield unto them that
put their trust in him.*
Proverbs 30:5

And such trust have we through Christ to God-ward:
Not that we are sufficient of ourselves to think any thing
as of ourselves; but our sufficiency is of God.
2 Corinthians 3:4–5

Overcoming Fear

Have not I commanded thee? Be strong and of a good
courage; be not afraid, neither be thou dismayed: for the
Lord thy God is with thee whithersoever thou goest.
Joshua 1:9

The Lord is my light and my salvation; whom shall I fear?
The Lord is the strength of my life; of whom shall I be afraid?
Psalm 27:1

I sought the Lord, and he heard me, and delivered me
from all my fears.
Psalm 34:4

The fear of man bringeth a snare: but whoso putteth his
trust in the Lord shall be safe.
Proverbs 29:25

Be not afraid of sudden fear, neither of the desolation of
the wicked, when it cometh.
For the Lord shall be thy confidence, and shall keep thy
foot from being taken.
Proverbs 3:25–26

*Say ye not, A confederacy, to all them to whom this people
shall say, A confederacy; neither fear ye their fear, nor be afraid.*
Isaiah 8:12

*For God hath not given us the spirit of fear; but of power,
and of love, and of a sound mind.*
2 Timothy 1:7

*There is no fear in love; but perfect love casteth out fear:
because fear hath torment. He that feareth is not made
perfect in love.*
1 John 4:18

Letting Go of the Past

*Brethren, I count not myself to have apprehended: but this
one thing I do, forgetting those things which are behind,
and reaching forth unto those things which are before,
I press toward the mark for the prize of the high calling of
God in Christ Jesus.*
Philippians 3:13–14

*The Lord is merciful and gracious, slow to anger, and
plenteous in mercy.*
He will not always chide: neither will he keep his anger for ever.
*He hath not dealt with us after our sins; nor rewarded us
according to our iniquities.*
*For as the heaven is high above the earth, so great is his
mercy toward them that fear [respect] him.*

*As far as the east is from the west, so far hath he removed
our transgressions from us.*
Psalm 103: 8–12

*For if our heart condemn us, God is greater than our
heart, and knoweth all things.*
*Beloved, if our heart condemn us not, then have we
confidence toward God.*
1 John 3:20–21

*And you hath he quickened, who were dead in trespasses
and sins;*
*Wherein in time past ye walked according to the course of
this world, according to the prince of the power of the air,
the spirit that now worketh in the children of disobedience:
Among whom also we all had our conversation in times
past in the lusts of the flesh, fulfilling the desires of the
flesh and of the mind; and were by nature the children of
wrath, even as others.*
*But God, who is rich in mercy, for his great love
wherewith he loved us,*
*Even when we were dead in sins, hath quickened us
together with Christ, (by grace ye are saved;).*
Ephesians 2:1–5

Prosperity

*Beloved, I wish above all things that thou mayest prosper
and be in health, even as thy soul prospereth.*
3 John 2

Keep therefore the words of this covenant, and do them,
that ye may prosper in all that ye do.
Deuteronomy 29:9

Only be thou strong and very courageous, that thou mayest
observe to do according to all the law, which Moses my
servant commanded thee: turn not from it to the right hand or
to the left, that thou mayest prosper whithersoever thou goest.
Joshua 1:7

This book of the law shall not depart out of thy mouth;
but thou shalt meditate therein day and night, that
thou mayest observe to do according to all that is written
therein: for then thou shalt make thy way prosperous, and
then thou shalt have good success.
Joshua 1:8

And in my prosperity I said, I shall never be moved.
Psalm 30:6

Peace

Thou wilt keep him in perfect peace, whose mind is
stayed on thee: because he trusteth in thee.
Isaiah 26:3

Peace I leave with you, my peace I give unto you: not as
the world giveth, give I unto you. Let not your heart be
troubled, neither let it be afraid.
John 14:27

These things I have spoken unto you, that in me ye
might have peace. In the world ye shall have tribulation:
but be of good cheer; I have overcome the world.
John 16:33

Therefore being justified by faith, we have peace with
God through our Lord Jesus Christ:
By whom also we have access by faith into this grace
wherein we stand, and rejoice in hope of the glory of God.
Romans 5:1–2

For to be carnally minded is death; but to be spiritually
minded is life and peace.
Romans 8:6

THE RENEWED MIND LIFESTYLE

The renewed mind lifestyle is a disciplined walk that requires focusing our thoughts on the scriptures in the Bible and not on the circumstances of the world. We can't always control what life throws in our direction. But we can control our responses to those challenging circumstances that try to throw us off balance. Whether it is a financial hardship, the death of a loved one, the loss of a job, a health issue, academic pressures, family problems, or the destruction of your home and property due to an environmental calamity, God is always there to help you pick up the pieces if you allow Him to.

There are over nine hundred promises in the Bible, and God wants us to claim each and every one of them. "God is light, and in Him is no darkness at all" (1 John 1:5). With the assistance of Bible classes that teach you the integrity of God's Word and how to operate the gift of holy spirit, and with a wonderful believing household that edifies and builds you up, there is no challenge in life that is too small or too big for God. God has given us all the resources that cause us to triumph in Christ. Our responsibility is to believe and act on the promises of God's Word.

Ephesians is one of the greatest revelations given to the Church of God. Ephesians represents the believer's heavenly standing in Jesus Christ. In his doctrinal epistle to the church, Paul admonishes the believers to stand and withstand against the pressures and onslaughts of the day. His admonition still holds practical keys today in resisting and standing against the wiles of the wicked one. As born-again believers, we have the privilege and the responsibility "to open their eyes, and to turn them from darkness to light, and from the power of Satan unto God, that they may receive forgiveness of sins, and inheritance among them which are sanctified by faith that is in me" (Acts 26:18). The following passage summarizes God's exhortation to the believer:

> *Finally, my brethren, be strong in the Lord, and in the power of his might.*
> *Put on the whole armour of God, that ye may be able to stand against the wiles of the devil.*
> *For we wrestle not against flesh and blood, but against principalities, against powers, against the rulers of the darkness of this world, against spiritual wickedness in high places.*
> *Wherefore take unto you the whole armour of God, that ye may be able to withstand in the evil day, and having done all, to stand.*
> *Stand therefore, having your loins girt about with truth, and having on the breastplate of righteousness;*
> *And your feet shod with the preparation of the gospel of peace;*

Above all, taking the shield of faith [believing],
wherewith ye shall be able to quench all the fiery darts of
the wicked.
And take the helmet of salvation, and the sword of the
Spirit, which is the word of God:
Praying always with all prayer and supplication in the
Spirit, and watching thereunto with all perseverance and
supplication for all saints;
And for me, that utterance may be given unto me, that I
may open my mouth boldly, to make known the mystery
of the gospel.
Ephesians 6:10–19

PRACTICAL KEYS TO
APPLYING THE BIBLE

1. Ask God to show you what you need to remove from your physical surroundings that is preventing you from thinking God's Word, being peaceful, and effectively operating the power of God.

2. Identify those mental habit patterns that you need to change that are contrary to the Word of God. For example, the Bible says, "Beloved, I wish above all things that thou mayest prosper and be in health even as thy soul prospereth" (3 John 2). Do you really believe God's Word? Or do you operate from a mind-set of lack and need rather than of prosperity and abundance? Begin to write down and memorize scriptures that deal with prosperity and health.

3. Be aware of the words you speak, which originate from your thought patterns regarding your finances, health, relationships, job, family, and your physical, emotional, mental, and spiritual well-being. Are the words you speak aligned with God's Word? If they are not aligned with God's Word, how would you go about changing your thinking so your words are biblically-based rather than circumstance-oriented?

4. Enlist the help of fellow believers to pray and believe with you for a positive outcome, whether the situation is a challenging health issue, finding a job, claiming God's prosperity in your life, helping you overcome fear, getting out

of debt, raising your children according to the principles of God's Word, or having peace in your life.

5. Feed your mind the spiritual nourishment of learning and applying principles from the Bible by enrolling in classes and study groups, listening to Sunday teachings, and reading magazines and literature that are based on the Word of God.

SCRIPTURES FOR FURTHER STUDY

1 Chronicles 29:11
Psalm 75:6–7
Psalm 98:1
Isaiah 25:8
Mathew 21:22
Romans 8:25, 28
1 Corinthians 15:51-58
Galatians 6:9
Ephesians 1:18–20
Hebrews 11:1
1 Thessalonians 4:15-18

APPENDIX 1

JESUS CHRIST

THE RED THREAD IN THE BIBLE

Genesis
Promised Seed of the Woman

Exodus
Passover Lamb

Leviticus
High Priest

Numbers
Star to Rise out of Jacob

Deuteronomy
Two Laws—Love God and Love your Neighbor

Joshua
Captain of the Lord of Hosts

Judges
Covenant Angel named Wonderful

Ruth
Kinsman Redeemer

Samuel
Root and Offspring of David

Kings
Greater than the Temple

Chronicles
King's Son

Ezra and Nehemiah
Rebuilder

Esther
Savior of God's People

Job
Daysman

Psalms
Song

Proverbs
Wisdom of God

Ecclesiastes
One Among a Thousand

Song of Solomon
Bridegroom of the Bride

Isaiah
Jacob's Branch

Jeremiah
Our Righteousness

Lamentations
Unbelievers' Judgment

Ezekiel
True Shepherd

Daniel
Stone that Became the Head of the Corner

Hosea
Latter Rain

Joel
God's Dwelling in Zion

Amos
Raiser of David's Tabernacle

Obadiah
Deliverer on Mount Zion

Jonah
Our Salvation

Micah
Lord of Kings

Nahum
Stronghold in the Time of Trouble

Habakkuk
Our Joy and Confidence

Zephaniah
Our Mighty Lord

Haggai
Desire of the Nations

Zechariah
Our Servant—the Branch

Malachi
Son of Righteousness

Mathew
Jehovah's Messiah

Mark
Jehovah's Servant

Luke

Jehovah's Man

John

Jehovah's Son

Acts

Gift of Holy Spirit

Romans

Believer's Justification

Corinthians

Believer's Sanctification

Galatians

Believer's Righteousness

Ephesians

Believer's Heavenly Standing

Philippians

Believer's Self-Adequacy

Colossians

Believer's Completeness

Thessalonians

Believer's Soon Glorification

Timothy
Faithful Man

Titus
Fellow Laborer

Philemon
Love of a Believer

Hebrews
High Priest for Sin

James
Royal Law

Peter
Pastor

John
He is as We Are

Jude
Beloved

Revelation
King of Kings and Lord of Lords

Source: http://www.christianblog.com/blog/blessings2you/
jesus-christ-the-red-thread-of-the-bible/

APPENDIX 2

RESOURCES

Barna Group
2368 Eastman Avenue
Unit 12
Ventura, California 93003
Phone: 805-639-0000
Website: www.barna.org

Christian Book Distributors
140 Summit Street
Peabody, Massachusetts 01960
Phone: 800-247-4784
Website: www.christianbook.com

The Pew Forum on Religion & Public Life
1615 L Street, NW Suite 700
Washington, DC 20036-5610
Phone: 202-419-4550
Website: www.pewforum.org

The Way International
P.O. Box 328
19100 East Shelby Road
New Knoxville, Ohio 45871
Phone: 419-753-2523
Website: www.theway.org

FILM

Refuge From the Storm
This film accurately depicts the spiritual competition we face on
a daily basis. The movie is based on a true-life story of a young
woman's complete deliverance from the powers of darkness.

Vista Films International
1800 Thibodo Rd. #230
Vista, California 92081
Phone: 760-643-0850
Websites: www.vistafilmsinternational.com
www.refugefromthestormmovie.com

NOTES

THE BIBLE AS THE STANDARD

1. "Hero of Flight 93 Honored," *The Times, May 5, 2002, A1.*

2. David Gibson, "The Bible: Revered and Unread," *The Times,* December 10, 2000, AA1–AA2.

3. Nancy Gibbs, "We Gather Together." *Time,* November 19, 2001, 38. Since 2001, a study by the Barna Group indicates that, in spite of an increase in religious activity since September 11, 2001, "the faith of Americans is virtually indistinguishable today compared to pre-attack conditions." See "Five Years Later: 9/11 Attacks Show No Lasting Influence on Americans' Faith" accessed September 23, 2012, *www.barna.org/culture-articles/148-five-years-later-911 attacks-show-no-lasting-influence-on-americans.* See also a recent study by the Barna Group on "The Emotional and Spiritual Aftermath of 9/11 and Boston" accessed September 7, 2013, *www.barna.org/barna-update/culture/626-the-emotional-and-spiritual-aftermath-of-9-11#,UnVheRCmZ3s.*

4. E.W. Bullinger, *How To Enjoy the Bible* (Ohio: American Christian Press, 1983), xiii.

5. It is not the intent of this book to provide an extensive description of figures of speech and Orientalisms that are used in the Bible. A figure of speech provides greater emphasis to the meaning of a scripture. There are approximately 217 figures of speech in the Bible. E. W. Bullinger refers to figures of speech as "the Holy Spirit's own markings of our Bibles" (p. vi). For figures of speech used in the Bible, see E. W. Bullinger, *Figures of Speech Used in the Bible* (Michigan: Baker Book House, 1968). For Orientalisms in the Bible, see Bishop K. C. Pillai, *Orientalisms of the Bible,* vols. 1 and 2 (Ohio: Mor-Mac Publishing Company, 1969 and 1974) and *Light Through an Eastern Window* (New York: Robert Speller & Sons, 1963). For a better understanding of Oriental customs, see James M. Freeman, *Manners and Customs of the Bible* (New Jersey: Logos International, 1972) and Bernita Jess, *On the Trail of Manners and Customs of the Bible* (Ohio: American Christian Press, 2009).

6. An example of a biblical research principle is that the Bible interprets itself in the verse, in the context, or in previous usage. It is estimated that 85 to 90 percent of God's Word interprets itself in the verse. See Victor Paul Wierwille, *Power For Abundant Living* (Ohio: American Christian Press, 1971), 145–206. Additional principles of biblical research can also be found in Bullinger, *How To Enjoy the Bible.*

7. Stephen Prothero, *Religious Literacy—What Every American Needs To Know—And Doesn't* (New York: Harper Collins Publishers, 2007), 60–61.

8. Robert G. Lee, ed., *The American Patriot's Bible—The Word of God and the Shaping of America* (Tennessee: Thomas Nelson, 2011),

I-22–23. See also John R. Thelan, *A History of American Higher Education* (Maryland: The Johns Hopkins University Press, 2004).

9. See Howard Fineman, "One Nation, Under … Who?" *Newsweek*, July 8, 2002, 20–25.

10. Quoted in *The Declaration*, Winter 1988, no. 4. The idea that God's hand was involved in the birth of this nation can be found in Peter Marshall and David Manuel, *The Light and the Glory* (Michigan: Fleming H. Revell, 1977). See also Josiah Benjamin Richards (comp. and ed.), *God of Our Fathers* (Pennsylvania: Reading Books, 1994) and Lee (ed.), *The American Patriot's Bible*.

11. Jim Jess, "The Declaration of Independence: Liberty Declared and a Republican Order Initiated," *The Declaration*, Spring, no. 10 (1991): 3.

12. *Quotations of Abraham Lincoln* (Massachusetts: Applewood Books), 21.

ATTRIBUTES OF GOD

1. A number of books have been written about Job. The author has found Victor Paul Wierwille, *God's Magnified Word* (Ohio: American Christian Press, 1977) to be particularly informative. In Chapter Three, "Job: From Victim to Victor," Wierwille writes that "God had the account of Job recorded for one major purpose: to show us the goodness of God and the badness of the Devil; to show us the perfection of God and the wickedness of the Devil; to show us that God is all good and that the Devil is

all bad. God desires all men to see His will, in contrast to the Devil's will," 29.

2. See Harold S. Kushner, *When Bad Things Happen to Good People* (New York: Schocken Books, 1981). Kushner posits an imperfect God by "permitting bad luck and sickness and cruelty in His world," 148. However, the notion of a spiritual adversary is never recognized within the context of his book.

3. See H. B. Kuhn, "God, Names of," Merrill C. Tenney (ed.), *The Zondervan Pictorial Encyclopedia of the Bible,* vol. 2 (Michigan: Zondervan Publishing House, 1975), 760–766 and Judson Cornwall and Stelman Smith, *The Exhaustive Dictionary of Bible Names* (New Jersey: Bridge-Logos Publishers, 1998), 83–91. See also A. W. Tozer, *The Attributes of God—A Journey Into the Father's Heart,* vols. 1 & 2 (Pennsylvania: Wing Spread Publishers, 1997, 2001).

4. The *Bible Promise Book—New International Version* (Ohio: Barbour Publishing, Inc., 1990).

5. Dayna Curry, Heather Mercer, and Stacy Mattingly, *Prisoners of Hope: The Story of Our Captivity and Freedom in Afghanistan* (New York: Doubleday, 2002).

6. For an extensive research study that examines religion and health, see Harold G. Koenig, Michael E. McCullough, and David B. Larson, *Handbook of Religion and Health* (New York: Oxford University Press, 2001).

7. Victor Paul Wierwille, *Christians Should Be Prosperous* (Ohio: American Christian Press, 1970), 3.

THE SPIRITUAL COMPETITION

1.   Quoted in Phil Kloer, "The Changing Faces of Satan," *The Times*, October 27, 2002, AA1.

2.   "Most American Christians Do Not Believe that Satan or the Holy Spirit Exist," Barna Group, posted April 10, 2009, accessed March 24, 2013, www.barna.org/faith-spirituality/260-most-american-christians-do-not-believe-that-satan-or-the-holy-spirit-exis?q=Satan+real.

3.   Andrew Delbanco, *The Death of Satan—How Americans Have Lost the Sense of Evil* (New York: Farrar, Straus and Giroux, 1995), 9.

4.   In the beginning, when Adam and Eve were created, they were of body, soul, and spirit. The spirit that was created within them gave them perfect communication with God. As a result of their disobedience, i.e., original sin in Genesis 3, they relinquished their perfect relationship and communication with God. The supreme power and dominion that Adam had on earth (Genesis 1:26) was then transferred to Lucifer, who became the "god of this world" (2 Corinthians 4:4). It took the life, death, resurrection, and ascension of Jesus Christ and the gift of holy spirit promised in Acts 1:8, and the manifestation of holy spirit via speaking in tongues in Acts 2:4, to restore humanity's perfect relationship with God. See chapter 17, "Thou Shalt Surely Die," in Victor Paul Wierwille, *Power for Abundant Living* (Ohio: American Christian Press, 1971), 249–268.

5.   Jesus informed his disciples in Matthew 15:24 that he was sent to speak God's Word to the "lost sheep of the house of Israel." See also Matthew 10:6 and Romans 15:8.

6. The Israelites were surrounded by pagan religious practices that included human sacrifice. The classic story of Abraham offering Isaac as a sacrifice to God in Genesis 22 illustrates the contaminating influence that these practices had on Abraham. For a discussion of this topic, see Victor Paul Wierwille, *The Word's Way* (Ohio: American Christian Press, 2001), 145–156 and Shalom Spiegel, *The Last Trial* (Philadelphia: The Jewish Publication Society of America, 1967).

7. Charles W. Conn, *The Anatomy of Evil* (New Jersey: Fleming H. Revell Company, 1981). See also Carl A. Raschke, *Painted Black* (New York: Harper & Row Publishers, Inc., 1990).

8. As a born-again believer, a Christian has five sonship rights. They are redemption, justification, righteousness, sanctification, and the ministry of reconciliation. See Chapter 23, "Knowing One's Sonship Rights" in Wierwille, *Power for Abundant Living*.

9. William Glaberson, "Nation's Pain is Renewed and Difficult Questions Are Asked Once More," *New York Times*, December 15, 2012, A18.

SENSE KNOWLEDGE
VERSUS SPIRITUAL KNOWLEDGE

1. Tithing is giving ten percent of your net income, and abundantly sharing is giving anything over ten percent of your income to the church, synagogue, mosque of your choice or to charity. The tithe was first practiced by Moses, who gave tithes to Melchizedek, King of Salem, in Genesis 14:18–20. Moses taught

God's people about the importance of the tithe in Leviticus 27:30, Numbers 18:28, and Deuteronomy 14:22–29. The benefits of tithing and the consequences of not tithing are clearly stated in Proverbs 3:9–10 and Malachi 3:9–11. Tithing, or the law of giving and receiving, is also mentioned in Luke 6:38, 2 Corinthians 9:6–8, and Hebrews 7:1-6.

2. G. M. A. Grube, trans., *Plato's Republic* (Indianapolis: Hackett Publishing Company, 1974), 168.

3. Ibid., 170–173.

4. Colin McGinn, *The Making of a Philosopher* (New York: Harper Collins, 2002), 63.

5. Daniel Goleman, *Emotional Intelligence* (New York: Bantam Books, 1995), 5, 26.

6. Victor Paul Wierwille, *The Word's Way* (Ohio: American Christian Press, 1971), 133–136. The phrase "burnt offering" is also used in Judges 11:31. Because of a commitment that Jephthah made to God to deliver him from his enemies, he would offer a "burnt offering" to God. The "burnt offering" turned out to be his only daughter. She committed to going up to the mountains for two months and ultimately returned to her father. When she returned, she dedicated her life by living in the temple and serving God. See also James M. Freeman, *Manners and Customs of the Bible* (New Jersey: Logos International, 1972), 170, and Bishop K.C. Pillai, *Light Through an Eastern Window* (New York: Robert Speller & Sons, 1963), 118–121.

7.   This is the figure of speech known as the idiom of permission. See E.W. Bullinger, *Figures of Speech Used in the Bible* (Michigan: Baker Book House, 1968), 823. It is never God's will for His people to suffer. A person cannot be protected if he/she consistently rebels and disobeys the will of God. In spite of our human weaknesses, God's grace and mercy can prevail, as evidenced when Moses interceded on the Israelites' behalf, God was able to pardon them of their transgressions (Numbers 14:1–20). God is long-suffering toward us, "not willing that any should perish, but that all should come to repentance" (2 Peter 3:9).

8.   For further discussion on human sacrifice, see William Whiston, trans., *The Works of Josephus* (Massachusetts: Hendrickson Publishers, Inc., 1987), 822–827.

9.   See "hospitality," in J. D. Douglas et al., eds., *New Bible Dictionary Second Edition* (Illinois: Tyndale House Publishers, 1962), 494–495.

THE GIFT OF HOLY SPIRIT

1.   In Hinduism and Buddhism, the law of karma refers to action; physical, verbal, and mental. In *The Word of the Buddha,* it states that "all beings are the owners of their deeds (karma), the heirs of their deeds: their deeds are the womb from which they sprang, with their deeds they are bound up, their deeds are their refuge. Whatever deeds they do—good or evil—of such they will be the heirs. And wherever the beings spring into existence, there their deeds will ripen; and wherever their deeds ripen, there they will earn the fruits of those deeds, be it in this life, or be it in the next life, or be it in any other future life." See Nyanatiloka, comp. and trans., *The Word of The Buddha* (Austin, Texas: Stephen Greenberg, 1973), 19.

2. See Victor Paul Wierwille, *Receiving the Holy Spirit Today* (Ohio: American Christian Press, 1982), 11–18.

3. Different records of devil spirit possession can be found in Mathew 9:33, Mark 1:34, Mark 6:13, Mark 7:26, Luke 4:33, Luke 4:35, Luke 8:27.

4. See Wierwille, *Receiving the Holy Spirit Today*, 133–165.

5. Ibid., 151.

6. Ibid., 35.

7. Ibid., 35-36.

8. Victor Paul Wierwille, *The Bible Tells Me So* (Ohio: American Christian Press, 1971), 43.

9. Dr. Mehmet Oz, "Healing With An Open Mind," *Parade Magazine*, November 30, 2003, 26-28. See also, Larry Dossey, *Healing Words—The Power of Prayer and The Practice of Medicine* (New York: Harper Collins Publishers, 1993), Claudia Kalb, "Faith and Healing," *Newsweek* (December 10, 2003), 44-56, Jerome Groopman, *The Anatomy of Hope* (New York: Random House, 2004), Herbert Benson with Marg Stark, *Timeless Healing—The Power and Biology of Belief* (New York: Scribner, 1996), Jeff Levin, *God, Faith, and Health* (New York: John Wiley & Sons, Inc., 2001), Harold G. Koenig, *The Healing Power of Faith* (New York: Simon & Schuster, 1999).

10. Wierwille, *Receiving the Holy Spirit Today,* 16–17.

11. In addition to the manifestations that Jesus operated, namely, word of knowledge, word of wisdom, discerning of spirits, faith (believing), workings of miracles, and gifts of healing, the greater works refer to the manifestations that Jesus did not operate; speaking in tongues, interpretation of tongues, and prophecy. The last three manifestations were not available until the day of Pentecost.

RENEWED MIND—THE KEY TO POWER

1. Henry David Thoreau, "Life Without Principle," *Atlantic,* October 1863. Quoted in Leonard Roy Frank (ed.), *Quotationary* (New York: Random House), 509.

2. Joseph H. Thayer, *Thayer's Greek-English Lexicon of the New Testament* (Massachusetts: Hendrickson Publishers, Inc., 2003), 325.

3. For a discussion of the distinction between soul and spirit, see Victor Paul Wierwille, *Power for Abundant Living* (Ohio: American Christian Press, 1971), 229–247.

4. James Allen, *As a Man Thinketh* (New York: Barnes and Noble, Inc., 1992), 2.

5. Ibid., 24–25.

6. See Walter B. Cannon, *The Wisdom of the Body* (New York: W.W. Norton & Company, 1939), Hans Selye, *The Stress of Life, revised edition* (New York: McGraw-Hill Company, 1984), Hans Selye, *Stress Without Distress* (New York, J.P. Lippincott Company, 1974), Jean Tache, Hans Selye and Stacey B. Day (eds.), *Can-*

cer, Stress, and Death (New York: Plenum Publishing Company, 1979). Current research suggests that stress can also cause premature cell aging. See Catherine Brady, *Elizabeth Blackburn and the Story of Telomeres* (Massachusetts: The MIT Press, 2007).

7. Herbert Benson, Julie Corliss, Geoffrey Cowley, "Brain Check," *Newsweek,* September 27, 2004, 45–47.

8. Alex J. Zautra, *Emotions, Stress, and Health* (New York: Oxford University Press, 2003), 36.

9. Walter B. Cannon, "Voodoo Death," *Psychosomatic Medicine,* (1957), 19, 183.

10. Herbert Benson, *The Mind/Body Effect* (New York: Simon and Schuster, 1979), 23. See also Robert Ornstein and David Sobel, *The Healing Brain* (New York: Simon and Schuster, 1987).

11. Paul Martin, *The Healing Mind - The Vital Links Between Brain and Behavior, Immunity and Disease* (New York: St. Martin's Press, 1997), 31.

12. Geoffrey Cowley, "Our Bodies, Our Fears," *Newsweek*, February 24, 2003, 43–49. Not everyone experiences the "fight or flight" syndrome. See S. E. Taylor, L. C. Klein, B. P. Lewis, T. L. Gruenewald, R. A. R. Grunung, and J. A. Updegraff. "Biobehavioral Responses to Stress in Females: Tend-and-Befriend, Not Fight-Or-Flight." *Psychological Review 107* (2000): 411–429. According to Dr. Laura Berman, a study at UCLA found that when women experience stress, they do not go into "fight or flight," but rather, experience the "tend and befriend" phenomenon. Women

turn inward and want to nurture and focus on friends and family. Quoted in Suzanne Somers, *The Sexy Years* (New York: Three Rivers Press, 2004), 134–135. Evidence linking psychological outlook and cardiovascular health can be found in Anne Underwood, "The Good Heart," *Newsweek*, October 3, 2005, 49–55.

13. Cowley, 47–48. See also Christine Gorman, "The Science of Anxiety," *Time*, June 10, 2002, 46–54. According to Gina Kolata, the research linking stress and cancer is inconclusive. See "Does Stress Cause Cancer? Probably Not, Research Finds," *New York Times*, November 29, 2005, F1, F6.

14. Victor Paul Wierwille, *The Bible Tells Me So* (Ohio: American Christian Press, 1971), 44–46.

15. Victor Paul Wierwille, *Christians Should be Prosperous* (Ohio: American Christian Press, 1970), 9–10.

16. Dale A. Mathews with Connie Clark, *The Faith Factor* (New York: Viking, 1998), 7.

17. Harold G. Koenig, Michael El. McCullough, and David B. Larson, *Handbook of Religion and Health* (New York: Oxford University Press, 2001), 53–59.

18. Ibid., 64–71.

19. Ibid., 58.

20. Don Colbert, *Deadly Emotions* (Nashville: Thomas Nelson Publishers, 2003).

21. Zautra, *Emotions, Stress, and Health*, 72, 244.

22. David Spiegel, "Emotional Expression and Disease Outcome," *The Journal of the American Medical Association,* 281, no. 14 (April 14, 1999): 1328–1329.

23. Claudia Wallis, "The New Science of Happiness," *Time*, January 17, 2005, A8-A9. See also Anne Underwood, "For A Happy Heart," *Newsweek*, September 27, 2004, 54–56. The field of positive psychology emphasizes positive subjective experiences such as well-being, satisfaction, happiness, optimism, hope, and faith, to name a few qualities. See Martin E. P. Seligman, "Positive Psychology, Positive Prevention, and Positive Therapy," in C. R. Snyder and Shane J. Lopez, eds., *Handbook of Positive Psychology* (New York: Oxford University Press, 2002), 3–9, Norman Cousins, *Anatomy of an Illness As Perceived by the Patient* (New York: W.W. Norton Company, 1979).

24. Allen, *As a Man Thinketh,* 20.

25. Jesus Christ was the perfect Passover Lamb who fulfilled the law of the Old Testament. He represents our perfect sacrifice for physical wholeness and the remission of sins. For further study on this topic, see Chapter 9, "The Broken Body and the Shed Blood" in Wierwille, *The Bible Tells Me So,* 75–92 and Victor Paul Wierwille, *Jesus Christ Our Passover* (Ohio: American Christian Press, 1992).

26. See Raphael Gasson, *The Challenging Counterfeit* (New Jersey: Logos International, 1966), Cindy Jacobs, *Deliver Us From Evil* (California: Regal Books, 2001), Ed Murphy, *The Handbook of*

Spiritual Warfare (Tennessee: Thomas Nelson Publishers, 2003), Joyce Meyer, *Battlefield of the Mind* (New York: Warner Books, 1995), and Derek Prince, *Spiritual Warfare* (Pennsylvania: Whitaker House, 1987). A biblically accurate depiction of the spiritual competition we are in is presented in the movie, *Refuge From the Storm*. For further information about the movie, see the Resources section of this book.

27. Aaron Beck developed the theory of cognitive therapy at the University of Pennsylvania in the early 1960s. The cognitive model asserts that distorted or dysfunctional thinking characterizes all psychological disturbances. Changing the person's thinking and belief system brings about emotional and behavioral changes in the individual. See Brad A. Alford and Aaron T. Beck, *The Integrative Power of Cognitive Therapy* (New York: The Guilford Press, 1997), Aaron T. Beck, *Love Is Never Enough* (New York: Harper & Row, 1988), and Judith S. Beck, *Cognitive Therapy: Basics and Beyond* (New York: The Guilford Press, 1995).

GENERAL INDEX

SCRIPTURE INDEX

25:37, 88
25:39, 88
2 Samuel
22:29–34, 136
1 Kings
15:14, 34
2 Kings
17:8–9, 79
17:16–17, 79–80
1 Chronicles
28:9, 77
29:11, 176
2 Chronicles
14:2-6, 33-34
15:2, 34
15:7, 34
Job
1:1–22, 23
2:9, 23
5:17, 23
9:24, 135
13:4, 147
16:2, 147
19:2, 147–148
24:13–14, 25, 54
27:5–6, 23
31:32, 86
31:35, 23
Psalms
1:1–3, 44, 143
5:4, 25
9:10, 63
9:17, 15
10:2, 60
19:12, 144
27:1, 168
28:7, 66
29:11, 29
30:6, 171
33:12, 15
34:4, 168
34:13, 150
34:19, 25
34:22, 25
35:27, 44

37:1-9, 17
37:3–6, 167
37:25, 63
37:32, 57
37:35, 62
37:40, 167
51:10, 144
51:11, 85
52:2–4, 149
53:1, 21
73:28, 167
75:6-7, 176
82:5, 57
84:11, 17, 19
98:1, 176
103:1-12, 17
103:8–12, 29, 169–170
106:21–28, 156
106:34–39, 58, 80
106:40-43, 80
107:20, 9, 37, 154
111:10, 22
118:8, 130
119:10–11, 144
119:16, 144
119:97–98, 136
119:105, 32, 136
119:160, 24
135:15–18, 20
138:2, 13
139:23–24, 144
143:10, 144
147:1-7, 44
147:5–6, 63
Proverbs
1:23, 85
2:6, 73
3:2, 31
3:5-6, 17, 68, 124, 167
3:5–8, 37
3:9-10, 191
3:25-26, 168
3:26, 34, 130
4:16, 57
4:23, 124

6:15, 88
6:16–19, 149
6:24–26, 148
12:6, 149
15:1–2, 40, 150–151
15:4, 151
15:23, 150
15:26, 150
16:5, 60
16:18, 52, 107
16:18–19, 59
16:24, 150
17:22, 133
17:27–28, 150
18:6–8, 148
18:21, 146
19:15, 161
20:11, 152
20:19, 148
21:23, 148, 151
22:4, 155
23:7, 124
24:10, 70
25:11, 151
27:17, 94
28:20, 8, 13, 143
28:26, 155
29:23, 155
29:25, 63, 107, 168
30:5, 167

Ecclesiastes
1:9, 55, 140
4:1, 62
9:11–12, 135

Isaiah
5:13, 56
5:20, 56
8:12, 66, 169
8:19–20, 108, 159
14:12–14, 50, 52, 156
14:15, 156
14:17, 52
25:8, 176
26:3, 11, 171
26:3–4, 29, 66

28:11–12, 112
47:9–15, 159
55:8–9, 104
57:3, 159
57:5, 80
58:7, 86

Jeremiah
7:31, 80
13:10–11, 78-79
15:16, 11
19:3–5, 78
32:27, 68

Daniel
3:5–6, 32
3:17, 33
3:25, 33
3:29, 33

Hosea
4:6, 56, 154
5:4, 57

Micah
5:12, 159

Nahum
3:4–5, 159

Malachi
3:5, 159
3:9-11, 191
3:10, 69–70
3:10–11, 39
3:11, 51

Matthew
2:16, 58
4, 60–61
4:1, 51
4:3, 51
4:8–9, 49–50
4:10, 50
4:16, 50
4:23, 37, 50
5:6, 92
6:33, 21, 38
9:20–22, 128
9:33, 193
9:35, 41
10:6, 99, 189

ABOUT THE AUTHOR

D r. Aleta You has spent thirty-two years in teaching and in the administration of higher education. In her professional career, she was an Associate Professor and Director of Student Teaching at Incarnate Word College, Assistant Director of the Teacher Preparation Program at Princeton University, and was a Senior Administrator at Rutgers University. After a productive and fulfilling career, Dr. You retired from Rutgers University in July 2013. She earned her bachelor's degree from Bradley University, her master's degree from the University of Hawaii, her PhD from Arizona State University, and did her postdoctoral work at the University of Texas at Austin.

In addition to her professional career in higher education, she currently serves as a Bible Household Fellowship Coordinator and continues to study, research, and teach the Bible. Since 1984, Dr. You has studied the Bible as well as countless philosophers and other religions until she found what were the answers to her spiritual longing. Her life's efforts and spiritual journey have informed her beliefs and served as an inspiration and guide to finding the powerful potential of God and His Word, which she shares in *Biblical Solutions for Daily Living - Developing a Vital and Personal Relationship with God.* For additional information about the author, please visit her at www.aletayou.com

Made in the USA
Charleston, SC
02 January 2015